# THE CHA...
# San Antonio

AN INSIDER'S VIEW OF AN
EMERGING INTERNATIONAL CITY

# Nelson W. Wolff

FOREWORD BY
HENRY CISNEROS

*Maverick Books*
*Trinity University Press*
SAN ANTONIO

Published by Maverick Books
an imprint of Trinity University Press
San Antonio, Texas 78212

Copyright © 2018 by Nelson W. Wolff

Book design by BookMatters, Berkeley
Cover image: © iStock.com/Shaun Pavone photo

Author photo courtesy of Bexar County

ISBN 978-1-59534-847-0 paperback
ISBN 978-1-59534-848-7 ebook

Trinity University Press strives to produce its books using
methods and materials in an environmentally sensitive
manner. We favor working with manufacturers that
practice sustainable management of all natural resources,
produce paper using recycled stock, and manage forests
with the best possible practices for people, biodiversity,
and sustainability. The press is a member of the Green
Press Initiative, a nonprofit program dedicated to supporting publishers in their efforts to reduce their impacts
on endangered forests, climate change, and forest-
dependent communities.

The paper used in this publication meets the minimum
requirements of the American National Standard for
Information Sciences—Permanence of Paper for Printed
Library Materials, ANSI 39.48–1992.

CIP data on file at the Library of Congress

22   21   20   19   18   |   5   4   3   2   1

# CONTENTS

*To my wife, Tracy:*
*the love of my life, my partner,*
*and a great mother and grandmother*

# *Foreword*

THE SAN ANTONIO AND BEXAR COUNTY region is prospering economically and experiencing a new level of social cohesion, which emanates from the expansion of opportunity. In the decade from July 2007 to July 2017, private sector jobs in the region increased by more than 170,000 jobs—a 24.3 percent increase, the third-highest rate of job growth among US metropolitan areas. That employment momentum has made possible unprecedented levels of social mobility, residential integration, leadership sharing, and cultural respect. The region is frequently highlighted in national media as a model of multicultural inclusion and cooperative decision-making for a nation that is increasingly diverse and in need of models of collaboration. But the relationship between San Antonio and Bexar County hasn't always been a model of harmony.

San Antonio and Bexar County have a long and storied history, and much of it has been as difficult, hot, and rough-edged as the climate and topography of the region itself, which sits astride the rocky outcroppings of the Texas Hill Country and the dusty scrublands of the Texas Brush Country. The region has been fought over, survived massacres and battles, and changed hands between nations several times. It has been home to indigenous hunter-gatherers, colonizing Spaniards, nation-building Mexicans, pioneering Americans, and ambitious immigrants from every part of the world. Each group in its turn has had to endure the elements, tame the land, defend its ground, and forge an economic rationale for a region. That struggle and progression has been marked by notable historical events, from the siting of campsites along the verdant San Antonio River thousands of years ago to the arrival of Spanish explorers in 1692, the establishment of a municipal government in 1718, the *municipio*'s designation as a northern anchor of the new nation of Mexico, the Battle of the Alamo in 1836, the city's role as the largest settlement in the Republic of Texas and the new American state of Texas, and its role as an American military fort in the aftermath of the Civil War.

That challenging march of civilization was steady enough that by the early 1900s San Antonio was being compared in national publications to such other frontier centers of civilization as New Orleans and San Francisco.

But then San Antonio started to slip behind the other growing cities of what is now the Texas Triangle. Over the decades, Houston determinedly dredged a fifty-two-mile ship channel and became the energy capital of the world. Dallas assembled banking and cultural institutions and started a building juggernaut that created the imperative for DFW Airport and a global role for the Metroplex. Austin steadily converted the assets of the state capital and the flagship University of Texas into a world-class technology and innovation complex. For a fifty-year span from the 1920s to the late 1960s, San Antonio was characterized as charming but an economic laggard, colorful but divided by its politics, and quaint but hobbled by poverty. The author Sidney Lanier, who lived in San Antonio during a period of convalescence, once wrote: "If peculiarities were quills, San Antonio would be a rare porcupine." By the 1950s the region's luxuriating in its distractions had produced an alarming scenario of civil strife, segregation, poverty, factionalism, inequality, and stalemate. A leading business and civic leader said in the *Wall Street Journal* that for San Antonio to be able to start over, the old order might have to burn to the ground.

From that nadir, the last fifty years have been a miraculous story of a region that looked into the abyss and didn't like what it saw. Leaders from every faction, social group, and ethnic heritage arrived at the same conclusion: things had to change. And since the mid-1960s change has been pursued with intentionality, leadership, tolerance, and foresight. The result has been a consensus built on two basic pillars: progressive economic development to grow jobs and wages, wealth and opportunities, and respect for social progress across rich heritages—indeed, a narrative that goes beyond people simply admiring each other's roots and is in fact a new blended culture that is, simply, San Antonio.

Together they constitute a better way of living together; and of governing together, learning together, praying together, and building a city together.

The person uniquely suited by his background and temperament to shepherd this process has been Nelson Wolff. His work as county judge is the culmination of the lessons, associations, and experiences of having served as a state representative, a state senator, organizer of a state constitutional convention, a businessman, a chair of a citywide goals process, and a successful mayor. At every step Nelson has understood and advanced the two pillars of governance in this era. Boiled down to their essence they are: grow the pie so it benefits everyone, and respect everyone's heritage and their right to have a place at the table.

Nelson Wolff has been the foremost public leader of the past twenty-five years in a region full of effective leaders. His contributions are on par with the greatest leaders of the region's history. His personal attributes have made the region's achievements possible. He has been determined, collegial, approachable, persuasive, and at once visionary and pragmatic.

His overarching achievement has been to transform the county government into a modern engine of competence in its basic responsibilities and catalytic investments for the future. That platform has then made possible many concrete projects over the past twenty-six years. The six initiatives reviewed in this book are examples of how public progress is created when continuity, steadiness, partnership, and the wise use of public finances are the governing principles. The initiatives touch on six core dimensions of the region's life: the identity of the San Antonio River, a modern arts venue, the region's preeminent health center, the judicial and corrections system, a technology innovation cluster, and accessible education.

It is hard to imagine a more broadly comprehensive and yet deeply impactful package of initiatives to have championed and explained for posterity.

Individually each of these initiatives creates a legacy unto itself, fundamentally advancing a sector of the city and county. Together they speak to the essence of why we band together to govern ourselves: to live, work, learn, and play together, and to find enrichment in our common humanity.

Nelson Wolff has done the heavy lifting for our region, mobilizing support for these initiatives, assembling the capital, and persuasively making the case to the public. By stopping to reflect on their beginnings and chronicling the evolution of each one in this important book, Nelson has performed an additional public service. He has taught us about the wisdom of public investments, helped us appreciate effective public leadership, and reminded us of our own stake in the region's future.

*Henry Cisneros*

## INTRODUCTION

# *Passing the 2008 Bond Issue*

IN MAY 2001 I WAS APPOINTED county judge by the Commissioners Court when Judge Cyndi Taylor Krier resigned to become a member of the University of Texas Board of Regents. The county judge is chair of the Commissioners Court and, along with four commissioners, is responsible for setting county policy and managing and funding county government.

After I assumed office it did not take me long to recognize that I was leading a very weird form of government, you might say a nineteenth-century relic residing in the backwaters of governance. It was a fragmented organization with legislative and state constitutional restraints, as well as a plethora of elected officials. The sheriff, district attorney, county and district clerks, constables, numerous judges, and tax assessor-collector were all elected.

Not only was county government fractured, but the Commissioners Court also made it worse by having some ten executives report directly to them. Many of them were there because of their political connection to members of the court. Some were simply incompetent.

It was so different than the City of San Antonio, where I served as mayor during the 1990s. San Antonio is a home rule city with a hierarchical management structure: straight lines of authority lead up to the city manager. The mayor is expected to set policy along with the city council and to direct the city manager and staff to carry it out.

As county judge, it would take me a few years to replace all the directors and hire top-notch people in their place. I was also able to consolidate additional power in my chief of staff, Seth Mitchell, by creating a county executive committee and naming him chair. After my son Kevin Wolff, a Navy veteran and former vice president of Citi Group, was elected to the Commissioners Court, I finally had the votes to appoint a county manager. In 2009 the court designated our budget director, David Smith, as county manager, setting up straight lines of authority. Smith had a master of science degree in finance from Louisiana State University and a master's in urban administration from Trinity University.

As a former mayor, I knew the power of the budget, and the Commissioners Court had that authority over all the functions of county government. While it took me a while to reorganize the bureaucracy, I would quickly learn how to use the budget to influence and direct progressive policies and a new vision. Within a year I was also able to gain the confidence of my four colleagues on the court and with their support began to move the county forward.

In my book *Transforming San Antonio*, published in 2008 by Trinity University Press, I highlighted four major initiatives that I led or participated in during my first seven years as county judge.

I participated in building the AT&T Center, home of the San Antonio Spurs and the San Antonio Stock Show & Rodeo. We completed these venues in 2003. Since then the Spurs have won four national championships. With increased revenue the rodeo was able to upgrade its talented performers and its stock. It has since been recognized yearly as the best indoor rodeo in the nation. Over one thousand people now work on the county grounds for Spurs Sports & Entertainment, the San Antonio Livestock Exposition, and the county.

As a former state representative and state senator, I had the experience to lead an effort to pass legislation that gave Bexar County the right to create special improvement districts in the unincorporated areas of the county. The first one we created was the Cibolo Canyon Special Improvement District. It had the authority to levy taxes to support the infrastructure needed to build a new community that included the 1,002-room JW Marriott San Antonio Hill Country Resort & Spa and two adjacent PGA golf courses. Today more than seven hundred people work at the hotel, the latest and by far largest resort destination in San Antonio. Under our agreement the developer Forestar set aside eight hundred acres of land and the county bought a 1,700-acre adjacent tract. Both will be preserved in their natural state forever. Environmental regulations on the development of the neighborhood have created a green, lush environment. Hundreds of homes have been built in conformity with the regulations.

Then Mayor Phil Hardberger and I teamed up to expand the River Walk north approximately 1.5 miles up to the twenty-two-acre Pearl Brewery redevelopment. From proceeds of selling Pace Picante, Kit Goldsbury developed a food theme to transform the Pearl Brewery into a multiuse development. Anchored by the Culinary Institute of America, there are some twelve chef-run restaurants. A 146-room boutique hotel, 480 apartments, and 30 retail and businesses are located on site. Hundreds of other living units have been built near the Pearl along the museum reach of the river.

Finally, I took the lead in working with Toyota officials to locate the Toyota automobile manufacturing plant in San Antonio. The plant opened in 2006, and today more than seven thousand people work for Toyota and its onsite suppliers.

If you read *Transforming San Antonio*, you may recall that I left readers hanging in the last chapter. At the time we did not know the outcome of the May 2008 venue election called by the Bexar County commissioners. In that election, we broke new ground by being the first county in Texas to propose using hotel-motel taxes and car rental taxes to build venues other than convention centers and professional sports stadiums.

I am telling this story because without the approval of voters in the 2008 election, two of the six initiatives I discuss here would not have happened—the Mission Reach of the San Antonio River and the building of the Tobin Center for the Performing Arts.

The bond election became the major turning point in Bexar County's transition into the twenty-first century. We embarked on the county's first major diversified initiative in its history and established Bexar County as a strong change agent in investing in legacy projects that would benefit future generations.

It began in a rather strange way. Because in 2000 the county had been conservative in its estimate of hotel-motel and car rental taxes to build the arena, we found that extending the term would give us some $400 million in new revenue. So in 2006 I made a run at getting the Florida Marlins major league baseball team to move to San Antonio. After working four months on the project, I came to my senses and realized they were lying about relocation so I dropped my solicitation.

But it was not in all vain. By carefully reading the state statutes, I learned that the hotel-motel and car rental tax could be used for various other purposes. No county or city in Texas had ever used these revenues in this way. I jumped on the chance.

Over several years there had been discussions within the arts community about building a true world-class performing arts center. The San Antonio Sports Association had studies in hand showing the need for more amateur sports facilities. The county, along with the San Antonio Spurs and the San Antonio Stock Show & Rodeo, wanted to make improvements to the Freeman Coliseum and the arena, and to add additional exhibit halls. The San Antonio River Oversight Committee needed funds for trails, portals to the missions, pavilions, and other amenities along the Mission Reach of the river. Each proposed initiative had a built-in and committed constituent base I could count on for support.

In late 2006, after many weeks of the various supporting groups lobbying my colleagues on the Commissioners Court, I was able to push for a vote to approve a process to consider four proposals for a bond issue. Because elements of all these projects were located throughout the county, each commissioner had much to gain: building a performing arts center, restoring the southern reach of the San Antonio River, building regional amateur sports parks, and improving the AT&T Center and the Freeman Coliseum.

In May 2007 we selected members of three task forces that would present their recommendations to the court by year's end. Each task force had approximately twenty members. San Antonio Area Tourism Council executive director Marco Barros and George Block, assistant director for Northside Independent School District, were chair and vice chair respectively of the

Amateur Sports Facilities task force. Former councilman Roger Perez became chair and Milton Guess vice chair of the River Walk extension task force. Symphony chairperson Debbie Montford and hotelier Henry Feldman signed on as chair and vice chair respectively of the Cultural Affairs task force.

Bexar County's Community Arenas Board, which included representatives from the Spurs and Rodeo, developed plans for the coliseum grounds and arena.

Mike Sculley, the former president of the Maricopa Sports Commission in Phoenix and husband of City Manager Sheryl Sculley, led the effort to organize the task forces.

But as the task forces began their work, strong opposition emerged from USAA's CEO Bob Davis and Bill Gold, president of Enterprise Rent-A-Car. They sent their representatives to our task force meetings questioning our right to use the car rental tax to build the proposed projects. They let it be known that they would oppose any extension of the tax. Commissioner Lyle Larson also raised objections to our moving forward.

But then we got lucky. In December the USAA Board of Directors announced that Davis had abruptly resigned. I was delighted when retired general Josue Robles became CEO. The *San Antonio Express-News* reported that employees burst into applause. Robles supported us, and USAA contributed $50,000 to the campaign.

Once Robles supported us, Gold and the car rental people folded their tent. We got another break when Commissioner Larson decided to run for Congress. Although he eventually voted to hold the election, he stayed neutral in the campaign. He went on to lose the congressional race but made a comeback later when he was elected to the Texas House of Representatives.

We were also very fortunate that my friend and fellow South

Sider the late Milton Guess represented the tourism industry. I had first worked with Guess when we began work on the Mission Trails Project while I was mayor. He was instrumental in convincing the hospitality industry to actively support the bond issue.

Eight months later, in January 2008, the task forces reported to the court. They recommended that four separate proposals totaling $414 million be submitted to voters. These included the performing arts center, thirteen regional sports parks, upgrades to the AT&T Center and the Freeman Coliseum, and the restoration of the Mission Reach of the river.

On January 22, 2008, the Commissioners Court voted on the four proposals. Commissioner Paul Elizondo amended the $110 million performing arts center proposal, shifting $6 million to the Alameda Theater restoration and $4 million for the Briscoe Western Art Museum. Commissioners allocated $85 million to the thirteen regional amateur sports parks, $125 million for the southern reach of the San Antonio River, and $100 million to the AT&T Center and the Freeman Coliseum. We voted 5–0 to place the initiatives on the ballot for the next election day: May 10, with early voting to start April 28.

Teaming up with Trish DeBerry and her public relations firm, we formed a political action committee named ACT (Athletics, Culture, and Tourism). We developed a media campaign, organized a grassroots effort, and made more than 1,200 presentations to civic organizations. On the election day of May 10, workers handed out literature at each polling station, and more than one hundred people walked door-to-door to bring out the vote.

On election night, Tracy and I joined hundreds of supporters at the Freeman Coliseum. We were nervous, but as the early vote came in, we relaxed. We were carrying the early vote, and we knew that when election day results came in, our lead would grow, because more progressive voters go to the polls on election day.

After all the returns were in, the Mission Reach gained 74.6 percent of the vote, followed by the sports facilities at 71.7 percent. The performing arts center, the Briscoe Western Art Museum, and Alameda Theater passed with 65.1 percent. The arena and coliseum passed with 56.9 percent.

Bexar County voter approval of the entire bond package had a huge economic impact on the city, leveraging an additional $400 million from partnerships we had formed on the projects. No other county bond issue ever had such a large diversity of projects or ever leveraged such a large sum of matching funds.

We have completed all thirteen amateur sports facilities. Our partners provided the sites, made additional investments, and now run the complexes. Including the partnerships, total investment was around $170 million.

At the Mission City Soccer Complex, the Classics Elite Soccer Academy, Culebra Creek Soccer Complex, and the STAR Soccer Complex, we built thirty-two soccer fields with parking, concession stands, restrooms, and other amenities.

We upgraded the baseball fields and concession stands at McAllister Park and made numerous other improvements. We built seven baseball fields, concession stands, and other amenities at Skyline Park and at the Missions Baseball Academy.

At the Mission Concepción Sports Park, we built a huge gymnasium—the only one like it in San Antonio—that can host six basketball games or twelve volleyball games at the same time. We also built four baseball fields and upgraded three other fields on the same site.

We partnered with Northside Independent School District to

build a fifty-meter, Olympic-size swimming pool, a twenty-five-meter diving and warm-up pool, and stands for 2,400 spectators.

We teamed up with St. Mary's University to build a 2,500-seat baseball stadium, a softball complex, a soccer field, and tennis courts. We built a fencing facility at the University of the Incarnate Word and soccer and track stadiums at the University of Texas at San Antonio (UTSA).

On the East Side, we built the Wheatley Heights Sports Complex that included three soccer fields, a stadium with a nine-lane track, a football field, grandstands, a concession stand, and other amenities.

The thirteen regional sports parks have enabled the city to attract numerous regional, state, national, and international amateur tournaments. This means more hotel room nights and car rentals. These facilities have provided first-class recreational outlets for all our citizens, young and old.

The AT&T Center and Freeman Coliseum proposal allowed for significant improvements on the 175-acre Bexar County grounds. We spent $75 million of the bond proceeds on the AT&T Center that leveraged another $30 million from the San Antonio Spurs. Improvements included a state-of-the-art sound system, six hundred video screens, a new center-hung scoreboard, upgraded Wi-Fi connections, new seats, and wider aisles. The center improvements also include additional space for a Whataburger store and an expanded fan gift shop. The Spurs lease was extended to 2032, assuring the team's presence in San Antonio for years to come.

We also upgraded the coliseum to include new seats, a new air-conditioning system, a new sound system, all new concession stands and concourses, and other building improvements. With the success of our new facilities, we partnered with the San Antonio Livestock Exposition to build 850,000 square feet of exposition halls.

With the exposition halls, the upgraded coliseum, and the extended lease with the Spurs, Bexar County entered a new area of economic activity on the 175-acre grounds as we attracted many conventions to our new exhibit space.

In the first two chapters of this book, you will read about the two transforming projects that were impacted by the voters' approval of the bond package in 2008: restoring the Mission Reach of the river, the quest for World Heritage designation for missions, and the beginning of the restoration of San Pedro Creek; and building the performing arts center. In later chapters you will learn about expanding the university hospital system; reforming the criminal justice system; going high tech; and creating Biblio-Tech, the nation's first all-digital public library.

# ONE

## The River, the Missions, and the Creek

MY TWO BROTHERS, GEORGE AND GARY, and I grew up on San Antonio's South Side in the 1940s and 1950s. We went to nine-cent Saturday afternoon matinees at the Highland Park Theatre, traded comics at a home-owned grocery store, played pick-up baseball games at Kite Field, played Little League baseball for G. S. McCreless Homebuilder's team, boxed at the Boys Club, and walked to Riverside Park Elementary School and then Page Junior High School.

With Mom and Dad, we attended many Missions baseball games at a great stadium right across Mitchell Street from Mission Concepción. The ballpark had replicas of the bell towers of Mission Concepción, so naturally that was our favorite mission.

We also had many good times exploring the banks of the San Antonio River. We fished, swam, and played on the green embankments. From an artesian well on the grounds of what is now University of the Incarnate Word, the clear, clean water joined with about a hundred other underground springs that flowed into the river. Olmos and San Pedro Creeks flowed into the river before reaching Mission Concepción, and Leon and Salado Creeks converged farther south.

The river took a meandering path when it reached the South Side. We often hiked along its banks, occasionally stopping to explore the four missions: Concepción, San José, San Juan, and Espada. We had a lot of fun prowling around the mission grounds looking for Indians and sticking our heads in the restored churches.

We knew from our school lessons that we were following the path of Native Americans who had lived along the river for some twelve thousand years. Some two hundred sub-bands of Coahuiltecans were later absorbed by other tribes. They all hunted, fished, gathered food, and camped along the river, eventually creating the village of Yanaguana.

They appear to have had a great life, one we would have enjoyed. But when the Spanish arrived and built the missions, that way of life changed dramatically.

Father Antonio de Olivares established the first mission, San Antonio de Valero, in 1718 along San Pedro Creek. The mission later moved to its present location and eventually closed in 1793. In 1801 soldiers turned the mission ruins into a fort that became known as the Alamo.

The other four missions were located south along the river. Father Antonio Margil de Jesús founded Mission San José in 1720. The other three missions—Espada, San Juan, and Concepción— were moved from East Texas to their present locations in 1731.

The missions spread over several miles because each had to be self-sufficient, and that required a lot of land. Just outside the mission walls were irrigated fields of crops and, beyond that, common grounds for grazing, hunting, gathering firewood, and acquiring building materials.

To support the crops, the Spanish built elaborate irrigation canal systems called acequias. The irrigation systems included seven dams to trap water and a system of irrigation ditches to deliver water from the San Antonio River to more than 3,500 acres of land.

When the missions were built, the Indians faced a serious lifestyle change. Priests at the Franciscan Catholic missions introduced the Indians to Christianity and Spanish culture and taught them to be farmers, ranchers, carpenters, and stonemasons.

For many decades, the mission way of life was vital both to the progress of Spanish settlement and to the integration of Native Americans into Spanish culture. But eventually the missions began a steady decline, and by 1824, all four had been closed. After one hundred years of mission life, the Native Americans were on their own.

The missions and the Alamo lay in ruins until the San Antonio Conservation Society and Daughters of the Republic of Texas (DRT) came to their aid in the early twentieth century. In 1902 the DRT, led by Adina De Zavala, began restoring the Alamo, which the state had purchased in 1883. The DRT preserved the ornate carved limestone façade, the traces of Native American frescos in the sacristy, and a portion of the Long Barrack. In 1924 the Conservation Society began a major effort to restore the four missions.

By the time my brothers and I were exploring the river in the 1940s and 1950s, the four missions and the Alamo had been stabilized. As we enjoyed the river, we had no idea about a plan hatched in Washington, DC, to destroy the southern reach of the river's habitat. The plan became public in 1954 when Congress authorized the US Army Corps of Engineers to begin a flood control project along thirty-one miles of the San Antonio River and its tributaries.

The Corps of Engineers is a federal agency within the Department of Defense that includes both military and civilian personnel. The Flood Control Act of 1936 gave it authority to build dams, levees, dikes, and other flood control projects. Subsequent flood control acts expanded its authority.

In order to better carry floodwater from the growing North Side of town, the Corps of Engineers decided to straighten the San Antonio River south of downtown. The engineers built concrete embankments in some places, denuded trees lining the banks, installed boulders and ripraps, and placed loose stones in the soft ground under the river. All this did tremendous environmental damage to the river and its embankments: by the early 1960s, the river had become an unsightly drainage ditch.

Although the river's terrible condition was ignored, 1978 brought one positive development for the four missions. Texan Senators John Tower and Lloyd Bentsen and US Representative Abraham "Chick" Kazen Jr. passed legislation creating the San Antonio Missions National Historical Park.

The legislation brought the four missions, a ranch, an aqueduct, and a series of archaeological sites on 862 acres under the administration and protection of the National Park Service. Forty-three historic structures were included in the park. The Alamo remained under the control of the state and the DRT.

Transferring the missions to the park service took five years to complete because a unique partnership had to be developed with the Roman Catholic Archdiocese of San Antonio. The archdiocese wanted to continue services in the four churches on the grounds of the missions. When it finally consented to be responsible for keeping the churches in good repair, the agreement was completed.

Even though the four missions were part of the park service, they did not draw many visitors. While I was mayor in the early 1990s, 4 million people visited the Alamo, but only 250,000 went to the other four missions. Experts said that the lack of a clear link between the Alamo and the other four missions was one reason for the low attendance.

As mayor, I took steps to enhance the linkage. I teamed with Henry Muñoz, then a member of the Texas Transportation Commission, to acquire highway enhancement funds to finance better connections among the missions.

In May 1993 we obtained a $200,000 planning grant from the Federal Highway Administration. The study focused on multiple routes to the missions, including bike and hiking trails, scenic corridors, pedestrian paths, and greenways.

With the study in hand, I convinced the city council in September to allocate $6.4 million to attract $14 million in state highway enhancement funds. The plan became known as the Mission Trails Project.

Along part of the main route on Roosevelt Street, the city buried CPS Energy power lines, installed street lamps, and built new sidewalks and a bus shelter. It also built new hike-and-bike paths along a segment of the river and in Espada Park, and made numerous other improvements to the street infrastructure.

While the Mission Trails Project created numerous improvements, the street pattern was just too confusing. Visitors had to drive down Alamo, St. Mary's, and Roosevelt Streets; Mission

Road; Padre Drive; Espada Road; and Ashley Road to reach the final mission, Espada, located about ten miles from the Alamo.

Many of us realized that the San Antonio River would be a better connecting link. So in March 1993 I convinced the city council to adopt a conceptual plan for the river put forward by the San Antonio River Authority (SARA). The plan called for river improvements from Guenther Street in the King William area south to Espada dam.

Later in December we expanded the plan to include improvements to the river from the Josephine Street tunnel inlet on the north edge of downtown south to Espada dam. But like many plans it did not include funding. Hence it was relegated to the back of the shelf where it sat for many years after I was term-limited out of office in 1995.

After taking office as county judge in May 2001, I was informed that Congress had passed legislation in 2000 authorizing the US Army Corps of Engineers to restore river ecosystems it had previously damaged. The corps was authorized to begin initial feasibility studies to explore the ecosystem restoration of channelized rivers. At last there was hope that the river of my youth could be restored.

We worked hard with our congressional delegation to become one of the first urban ecosystem restoration projects. In September, four months after my being appointed county judge, the corps received funding to begin a feasibility study of the ecosystem restoration of the eight-mile section of the river between Roosevelt Park and Mission Espada.

While the corps was conducting the feasibility study we partnered with the city to restore a one-mile segment of river from the Blue Star Arts Complex on Alamo Street to Roosevelt

Park where the Mission Reach, the eight-mile federal restoration project, would begin. The project, known as the Eagleland Reach, would serve as a pilot ecosystem restoration project for the corps. In 2003, two years after I took office, the Commissioners Court joined the city council to fund the $8.8 million project.

Along with the city, we contracted with SARA to manage the project. Created by the Texas legislature in 1937, SARA was responsible for the cleanliness and flow of the river. Its taxing authority was limited to technical planning, operations, and maintenance, leaving local funders responsible for capital projects along the river.

On January 7, 2004, Mayor Ed Garza and I kicked off the Eagleland Reach river project. It included removing the concrete channel; building a small overflow dam, called a weir, to form pools of water; creating rock and riffle waterfalls; planting native grass, flowers, and cypress trees; and building hike-and-bike trails. It became a visible example of what the eight miles of river from Roosevelt Park to Mission Espada could become.

Three months later, in April, the Army Corps of Engineers formally released its national environmental restoration plan for the eight-mile stretch of the river that became known as the Mission Reach because of the four missions along its banks. The corps wanted to do the restoration if Congress provided the funding.

So we began knocking on Washington's door to seek funding for the design stage. First we turned to Senator Kay Bailey Hutchison, who had been one of my colleagues in the Texas House during the early 1970s. I enjoyed serving with her, and I was also good friends with Representative Ray Hutchison, whom Kay married in 1978. Kay was elected to the Senate in 1993 during my term as mayor. She became a strong voice for San Antonio's military installations and our river. Through a congressional earmark, she obtained federal funding to begin design work of the Mission Reach.

While we were seeking federal funding for the Mission Reach, my great friend Phil Hardberger was elected mayor in May 2005. He immediately launched his boat and started paddling hard, but instead of going south, he headed north. He did not have to deal with the Army Corps of Engineers because the river going north was not part of ecological restoration.

The Commissioners Court agreed to help fund the project because it was an important section of the river that would lead to urban development along the river. We entered into an interlocal agreement with SARA to build the 1.5-mile Museum Reach to the Pearl Brewery redevelopment site. Of the nearly $71 million needed, the city put up $51 million, the county added $13 million, and the San Antonio River Foundation provided the remaining $6.5 million for artwork.

Meanwhile the Mission Reach remained a concrete ditch. The project did move one step forward in 2006 when the Corps of Engineers agreed to share responsibility with SARA, but, like the corps, SARA had no money.

Suzanne Scott, SARA's assistant general manager, and I met with officials from the Office of Management and Budget (OMB) and the Army Corps of Engineers in Washington, DC, in March 2006. But sadly, we found out that we would not receive any funding for construction of the project. The only source of federal funding would be for design and any annual congressional earmark that Senator Hutchison could obtain and those would only be in small amounts in relationship to the huge cost of the project. Later that year the Corps of Engineers announced that 30 percent of the design work on the Mission Reach was complete and that construction could start the next year on the first one-mile section if funding were available. In November, however, the OMB sent a letter to the corps stating that the project would be a low priority for any funding. After we failed to secure federal funding other than congressional earmarks, we knew that federal funding for the project was not going to be available.

I knew that unless the Commissioners Court stepped up with funding, the Mission Reach project never would be completed. We took our first step in 2007 when we developed a ten-year, $500 million plan for flood control, using a special flood control tax that the Texas legislature had authorized. It was a bold step for the county to take on such a large undertaking.

The financing plan was developed by our then-budget director, David Smith. David was a Trinity University graduate with a degree in urban administration. He started working for the county's budget department in 1997. The Commissioners Court appointed him in director in 2004; he would prove one of our best new appointments.

I teamed up with the senior member of the court, Paul Elizondo, to convince our colleagues to move forward with the plan. Commissioner Elizondo had served in the Marine Corps and afterward had taught in the Edgewood Independent School District. He was first elected to the legislature in 1978 and served two terms, and then was elected to the Commissioners Court in 1983. We developed a close friendship and would work together on numerous projects through the years.

The flood control funding was necessary because Bexar County was prone to flooding, with 1,100 linear miles of creeks and rivers that flow from north to south. Devastating flash floods in 1998 and 2002 killed eleven people and damaged more than 1,800 homes. The flood control projects included a series of regional dams, levees, reservoirs, low-water-crossing improvements, and floodplain buyouts.

The ten-year flood control plan approved by the court included flexibility for the Commissioners Court to add or take away projects depending on whether their final design was cost effective. Most importantly the plan provided the flexibility to add fund floor control elements in the Mission Reach of the river. While the funding could be used for flood control portions of the Mission Reach, it could not be used for amenities such as sidewalks and trails.

The year 2007 was also pivotal for SARA when the organization promoted Suzanne Scott to general manager. After receiving an MS in urban administration from Trinity University, Suzanne took on leadership positions at VIA Metropolitan Transit, the county, and then SARA.

I was delighted she was promoted, because she respected and understood the county. During the four years she had worked for Bexar County as the planning and policy manager, she led the effort to renegotiate a contract with SARA. We would become fast friends and forge a tight partnership.

On July 25 we put our oar in the river. The Commissioners Court appropriated $21.6 million to be advanced to the Corps of Engineers so they could get started on the 1.2-mile first phase of construction of the Mission Reach.

As planning continued for the remaining seven miles of the Mission Reach, cost estimates kept increasing. The Corps of Engineers, having never done a restoration, found the project was much more complicated and expensive than expected.

Matters got worse when congressional earmarking came to a halt. In April 2008, Citizens Against Government Waste listed the San Antonio River project in its Pig Book for unneeded parochial projects. That move was stupid and wrong, but it put Hutchison in a bad political position. In the design stage of the Mission Reach, she had been instrumental in keeping the project alive through congressional earmarks. Those would no longer be available.

In the introduction of this book I wrote about the approval by voters in May 2008 to provide $125 million in funding for amenities along the Mission Reach. Specific amenities along the river, including pavilions, benches, picnic areas, hiking, walking, and biking paths, were recommended by the River Oversight Committee, cochaired by former mayor Lila Cockrell and architect Irby Hightower. They also recommended funding portals to the four missions to make the river the connecting link and front door to the missions. As a result of the successful election, we now had funding for the proposed amenities.

The following month, after the bond election on June 2, we held a groundbreaking ceremony for the Mission Reach's first 1.2-mile segment from Lone Star Boulevard to the river's confluence with San Pedro Creek near Mission Concepción. This was the segment that the Commissioners Court had already prefunded so the work by the Corps of Engineers could begin.

While voters had approved the $125 million funding for the Mission Reach, we were still short of covering the cost of the whole project, including the flood control portion. We also had management problems. Too many entities were trying to steer the boat. The San Antonio River Foundation, the River Oversight Committee, the city, SARA, and the Corps of Engineers were all pushing and pulling, sometimes in opposite directions.

Before we appropriated funds for the river, the Commissioners Court wanted a clear line of authority, with us at the top. We wanted SARA, rather than the Corps of Engineers, to be in charge of construction because we believed SARA could construct the project for far less money. The court also wanted SARA to provide an accurate cost estimate and a timeline for completion, as well as a commitment to operate and maintain the project after it was completed. Together, we would also need to develop a management plan for the river after the work had been completed.

Early in 2009 SARA executive director Scott and I met to work out a plan of action. "Can we get the Corps of Engineers to turn over the construction of the project to you?" I asked.

"We are talking to them," she replied. "I believe they will, because they know Congress is not going to fund the completion of this project. They know the funding will have to come from the county, and they also know we can do it for less. We could save close to $24 million by eliminating the overhead cost of the corps."

"Tell them county funding is contingent on SARA managing the project," I replied. "Can you give us an accurate estimate of what it will take to finish if you get control of project?" She said yes.

I said, "We are willing to commit an additional $75 million in flood control funds. With the voter approval funds the total would be $200 million. We would want the right for the Commissioners Court to sign off on the design of the amenities, the priority of funding, and any contracts."

She agreed. I then asked, "What about the San Antonio River Foundation? I know you have had trouble with them when they've tried to second-guess SARA and the county. I met with them and they wanted a greater role in leading the project. After all their demands, including control of the funds we are providing for the portals to the missions, I got angry and told them we didn't need the foundation's help. They were a pain."

She nodded. "SARA created the foundation in 2003 and we had a great relationship until they hired Kim Abernethy in 2007. They then decided they wanted to expand their role and establish branding and communication efforts to exert control and decision-making authority beyond SARA's original purpose. They need to focus on raising funds for artwork instead of trying to tell SARA and the county what to do."

I said, "We will need to stiff-arm them and anyone else who tries to steer this boat."

"We will do it together," she agreed.

After that critical meeting, we began to make progress in consolidating power with SARA and the county. But the foundation continued to give Suzanne trouble until SARA's board decided to change the administrative support for the foundation and possibly sever ties with the foundation.

The river foundation got the word. Sonny Collins, board member and chair from 2006 to 2009, took the lead in removing the executive director and setting a pathway to creating an organization that would be collaborative and effective. Collins was a graduate of Alamo Heights High School and the University of Texas. He went on to a successful career in financial management in New York. He came back to San Antonio in 2003.

Board member Estela Avery was chosen to be the executive director. Estela is the wife of James Avery, who founded James Avery Jewelry in 1954. Today the firm operates five manufacturing plants and sells jewelry all over the United States. Under her leadership the foundation stuck to the purpose for which it was created. She took no salary and also gave the foundation $1 million.

The county joined hands with SARA and convinced the Corps of Engineers to turn the project over to them. SARA would have to follow the corps' design for the project, but the corps' oversight was minimized. We were ready to move the project forward with local control. After reviewing SARA's new cost estimates, we were confident that the Mission Reach could be completed with a county commitment of $200 million.

In June 2009 the Commissioners Court voted to commit the additional $75 million in flood control funds, along with the $125 million from the visitor tax. We then contracted with SARA, giving the Commissioners Court the right to sign off on various aspects of the construction project.

After the commissioners' vote, the *San Antonio Express-News* editorial page, under the leadership of Bruce Davidson, wrote that the county had ensured the completion of the Mission Reach. It also supported SARA's takeover of the project's management.

While the editorial board supported the action, a couple of misinformed reporters began to write negative stories. They alleged that the county's financing was built on a house of cards.

I called the newspaper's editor, Robert Rivard, and told him that interest rates were rapidly falling after the national financial implosion of November 2008, while, at the same time, construction prices were falling. These events allowed us to fund the flood component of the Mission Reach and not diminish other flood control projects.

Unfortunately, that did not stop the negative stories.

In August 2009 we sold county bonds to cover the cost associated with the Mission Reach and other flood control projects. The reporters finally shut up.

Also in 2009, the Commissioners Court directed staff to work with other agencies to develop a River South Management Plan. The city, SARA, the National Park Service, and the county agreed to develop a plan that would include maintenance, regulations, law enforcement, recreation, education, and economic development along the river corridor and adjacent areas. They would work with other public agencies, nonprofits, and neighborhoods to coordinate the various functions.

That same year, we got a little unexpected help from friends in Washington, DC. In response to the November 2008 economic fallout, President Barack Obama persuaded Congress to pass a large stimulus bill. We hoped to get $69 million in stimulus funds for the Mission Reach that would allow us to add other amenities, but ended up with $25.4 million.

As 2010 got under way, we got off to a quick, smooth start on the next segments of the Mission Reach. While the Corps of Engineers was completing the first 1.2 miles, Zachry Construction Corporation won the bid for the second one-mile segment. The bid came in at $22 million, 35 percent less than the corps had estimated.

With local funding in hand, SARA recommended that the remaining 5.75 miles of the project from Mission Road to Mission Espada be put out to bid to save money and time. In July Zachry, under the leadership of David Zachry, bid $99 million for this remaining work—$25 million under budget. This segment included relocating 2 million cubic yards of soil, 16 riffle structures, 10 acres of wetlands, and 250 acres of native vegetation.

With SARA in charge of construction, we had quickly proved

that we could save a huge amount of money. I now knew we would finish the project within the budget.

## THE QUEST FOR WORLD HERITAGE

As work proceeded on the Mission Reach, a parallel effort was under way to designate the missions as a World Heritage Site. Our efforts began in 2006 when Virginia Nicholas, whom I had appointed chair of the Bexar County Historical Commission, introduced the idea. She formed a committee that included Félix Almaráz, a UTSA history professor; Paula Piper, chair of the San Antonio Conservation Society; Susan Chandoha, executive director of Los Compadres; and Susan Snow, an archeologist for San Antonio Missions National Historical Park. They asked Paul T. Ringenbach, vice chair of the historical commission, to draft papers to support the nomination.

In summer 2007 the committee submitted an application to the Office of International Affairs of the National Park Service. In 2008 fourteen sites, including the Alamo and missions, were put on a tentative list by the National Park Service to submit to UNESCO. But we did not make the cut. The committee tried again in 2011, but again the National Park Service decided not to submit the nomination.

It would take some political muscle to move the nomination forward. And the guy to do that was Henry Muñoz. He was a friend of Interior Secretary Ken Salazar, a Democrat from Colorado who oversaw the National Park Service. Muñoz was also a member of the National Park Foundation Board. I had worked with him during the time I was mayor when as a member of the Texas Department of Transportation he provided funding to help link the missions through the Mission Trails Project.

Muñoz and I met with Salazar on two occasions in Washington, DC. As a former US senator (2005–2009), Salazar understood Washington politics and was sensitive to the concerns of political leaders. We had complained to him about the lack of support from the National Park Service for having the Alamo and missions declared a World Heritage Site. We told him that on two previous occasions we had submitted an application to the park service, but it had not forwarded a favorable recommendation to UNESCO.

We also told him about our work restoring the river and the portals we were building to the missions, and about the archdiocese's work to restore the churches at the four missions. Salazar told us he would personally look into it. We invited him to our June 2011 ceremony celebrating the first two miles of the river project.

On June 25 we gathered on the Theo Street bridge near Mission Concepción to celebrate the completion of river improvement and trails from Roosevelt Park to Mission Road. People gathered under a large tent in the middle of the bridge, mariachis sang, and, as master of ceremonies, I introduced Salazar.

After praising the environmental restoration of the river and recognizing how completion of the river project would link the historic missions, he said the magical words: "I will support the nomination of the four San Antonio missions and the Alamo as a World Heritage Site."

While we had worked hard to present a good case for the nomination, it took a personal political connection to get us in the game. Without Muñoz's connection to Salazar, we would never have made it to first base.

If they were designated a World Heritage Site, the Alamo

and missions would join such sites as the Statue of Liberty, Independence Hall, and the Taj Mahal. The missions and the Alamo would become the only World Heritage Site in Texas.

In September we celebrated another step the Commissioners Court had taken to support the missions. We provided $3 million to fund a demonstration farm at Mission San Juan to create a living-history component through the restoration of an acequia, a farm field, a barn, fencing, trails, and parking. Mayor Julián Castro and Hutchison joined me at Mission San Juan to open the sluice gate to allow water to flow from the restored acequia to the fields of the demonstration farm. The acequia provided water for seventy acres of farmland.

Scholars from Spain, Mexico, Canada, Cuba, Italy, and across the United States visited San Antonio in May 2012. They came to attend an international symposium of the US National Committee of the International Council on Monuments and Sites. If the National Park Service nominated the Alamo and missions as a World Heritage Site, this organization would decide whether to support the nomination before the World Heritage Committee. After discussion, they all agreed that the missions had "outstanding universal value." This was a very positive statement.

After the symposium, we hosted a dinner for the delegates under a large tent at Mission San José. Salazar and John L. Nau III, vice president of the National Park Foundation board, attended. Nau was also the chairman of the Texas Historical Commission and had played a major role in providing us grants to restore our historic courthouse. He would later play a role in supporting our nomination.

As master of ceremonies, I again introduced Salazar. By now we had become friends, and he related to me the obstacles we had to overcome to be nominated by the park service. He said he would keep up the pressure.

During his speech, he said the missions were an important and often overlooked chapter in this nation's history. He emphasized the need to better communicate the significance of the missions in blending the Native American and Spanish cultures.

The next morning, standing outside Mission Concepción, I pointed out to Salazar the Mission Concepción Sports Park that was under construction. The Catholic archdiocese had provided three hundred acres of land near the mission and adjacent to the river. The county invested $16 million to build the facility. In its first year more than 1 million people would attend the sports park.

We then had a press conference in front of the mission where Salazar announced that the nomination was being prepared to move forward to UNESCO. He said the missions were "truly a crown jewel of Americans' history and American heritage."

Even with Salazar's support, the application faced a review panel of governmental agencies to determine if it met UNESCO standards. The National Parks Conservation Association (NPCA) began a letter-writing campaign. In a very short time, more than eighteen thousand letters were sent to the National Park Service. The support was so overwhelming that the NPCA was asked to stop having emails and letters sent.

## THE FINAL STAGES OF THE MISSION REACH

While work continued on the World Heritage nomination the Mission Reach began to take shape. In 2012 four miles of the Mission Reach were completed several months ahead of schedule. We celebrated the accomplishment of reaching the halfway mark with a parade, led by Commissioner Sergio "Chico"

Rodriguez and me, launching the first kayaks and canoes on the river.

I spent more time along the river. I had bought a bicycle, which I kept in my office at the courthouse. I would ride to the river through the King William neighborhood; past South Town, the Blue Star Complex, Brackenridge High School, Roosevelt Park, and Mission Concepción; up to Mission Road and Riverside Golf Course, where the trail came to a temporary end. I would then park the bike and hike along the river, watching the work under way.

Construction workers were relocating millions of cubic yards of soil and building riffle structures, sidewalks, benches, pedestrian bridges, and pavilions. They were creating wetlands beside the river, laying irrigation lines, and planting native vegetation.

I stopped one day at the ruins of the once-famous Hot Wells Resort and Spa, located on the river across from Mission County Park. The 190-room resort hotel opened during the 1890s and became famous for the 103-degree sulfur water flowing from a 1,750-foot-deep well. Because of the thermal water, which was pumped into two elaborate bathhouses and marketed as medicinal, the rich and famous came to the resort. They included actors Rudolph Valentino and Sarah Bernhardt, Mexican president Porfirio Díaz, and President Teddy Roosevelt.

I had been talking with local developer James Lifshutz, the site's owner, about a possible donation to the county. It took us several years to reach an agreement with Lifshutz, but we finally did. As this book goes to press we are creating an entrance from Presa Street over the railroad tracks, stabilizing the ruins, creating an interpretive center, and landscaping the site down to the river. The Hot Wells Conservancy, led by Cindy Taylor, former president of the South Side Chamber, and Yvonne Katz, former superintendent of the Harlandale Independent School District, will manage the site and raise funds to restore the one remaining historic building.

As I rode the river I began spending time with Lee Marlowe, SARA's national resource management specialist, who chose the Texas native plants that were being reintroduced. Her team planted more than sixty species, such as Indian blanket, sunflowers, bluestem grass, and prairie wild rye on top of biodegradable erosion mats, as well as some forty-four types of trees and shrubs. The team used temporary irrigation hoses to water the plants for the first two years.

Marlowe helped me plant a wolfberry shrub, an extraordinary little plant with a vigorous root system that provides nitrogen to the soil. It has small flowers and tiny, edible silver berries. I was proud to share the plant's name.

Wildlife was returning to the river. On my bike rides, I passed herons, egrets, wood ducks, owls, turtles, black-bellied whistling ducks, woodpeckers, warblers, and flycatchers. SARA also stocked the river with native Guadalupe bass.

On February 12, 2013, the Commissioners Court approved the initial River South Management Plan. San Antonio police and park rangers would provide the bulk of security and law enforcement. SARA would be responsible for operations, recreation, and maintenance. SARA, the river foundation, and the National Park Service would handle education. The city and county were responsible for economic development.

One day in February, as I rode my bike farther down the river, the trail stopped at Padre Park. I followed a path up to the street and eventually found my way back down to the river. When I returned to my office, I called Scott to ask why. She told me that the River Oversight Committee had given in to demands from the Symphony Lane neighborhood not to build a trail in front of the neighborhood.

All the other neighborhoods had supported the trail, and this was the only section with a gap. I said, "We promised the voters a trail all along the river. Build the damn trail." She did.

*Express-News* columnist Brian Chasnoff wrote that my remarks were "not terribly charming, perhaps—but definitely effective."

The river restoration was nearing completion when an unforeseen event hit hard. Rain started falling in the early morning hours of May 25. A record rain, up to fifteen inches within five hours, was concentrated in the Olmos Basin, which flows into the San Antonio River.

The National Weather Service sent out an advisory warning at 4:04 a.m. and within two hours issued a flash flood warning. The rain was described as one for the ages.

By the time of the flash flood warning, Commissioner Rodriguez and I were touring the river to see how it was holding the water. We stood at the edge of Mission County Park watching the water rage south at 80,000 cubic feet per 4 seconds just a few feet below us. While the rushing waters had risen some 32 feet in the Mission Reach of the river, the river banks held the water. The Corps of Engineers had done a great job designing flood control for the river.

We did have flooding south of the river improvements in an area that had been previously designated a flood zone. We set up an incentive plan to buy property and assist owners in moving out of the flood zone.

The raging waters caused some damage on embankments in

the curves of the river. The plants and trees held up, except for a few recently planted ones. Insurance covered part of the damage, but the county still spent about $1 million for repairs.

Finally, some twenty years after presentation of the initial plan for the river improvements dating back to the time I was mayor, the day arrived to celebrate the completion of the Mission Reach. On October 5, 2013, a beautiful Saturday morning, supporters gathered in a pavilion on the river near the renovated Mission County Park. In the park, we had built sidewalks, lighting, restrooms, pavilions, parking lots, and a children's play area, as well as installing paving and grass. Adjacent to the park, we built a portal to Mission San José that provided people a great view of the mission.

In my remarks at the ceremony, I noted that with county, city, National Park Service, and riverside habitat, the Mission Reach now has more than 2,400 acres of parkland, about two and a half times the size of Central Park in New York City. I described how the environmental restoration would grow in elegance as the years passed—how future generations will see some twenty-three thousand saplings we planted stretch up to the sky as magnificent trees, reaching their final maturity in some fifty years.

We had now completed sixteen miles of trails, eighty-nine park benches, 137 picnic tables, five overlooks with shade structures, nine water-edge landings, six footbridges, four pavilions along the river, and four portals to the missions. The restoration included 13 acres of wetlands; 113 acres of aquatic habitat, some with restored riffles, runs, and pools sequences; and 334 acres of riparian habitat planted with more than ten thousand pounds of native grass and wildflower seeds of more than sixty species. It is anticipated that more than twenty-three thousand trees and shrubs of more than forty native species will be established over time. Recreation features included more than sixteen miles of hike-and-bike trails and eight miles of paddling trails.

The opening included a daylong celebration along the river, with three concurrent music festivals, fishing clinics for kids, a flotilla of boats sailing down the river, and guided kayak tours. What a grand day in the life of San Antonio!

The final cost for the eight-mile Mission Reach was $271 million. The county's share was $196 million. County savings from SARA's takeover of the project was reinvested in additional trails, canoe chutes, and other amenities. The county also reallocated $8 million to the Medal of Honor portal next to Tobin Center for the Performing Arts and $2 million to a portal for the Briscoe Western Art Museum. The balance of the $271 million came from federal funds ($57.9 million), the San Antonio Water System ($5.9 million), the city ($6.8 million), and the river foundation ($4.7 million). Had the Commissioners Court not stepped up, the Mission Reach never would have been completed.

While the county provided some 75 percent of funding and oversight, SARA managed the project and did the day-to-day hard work. Scott did a great job leading SARA.

With work completed on the eight-mile Mission Reach, the river improvements now extended all the way from Brackenridge Park to Mission Espada, a total of fifteen miles of waterway including the two-mile bend of the river downtown. The county contributed $230 million to the total river project cost of $384.1 million.

## WORLD HERITAGE DESIGNATION

With the completion of the Mission Reach, less than two years remained before the meeting of the World Heritage Committee of

UNESCO to decide on new inscriptions. Local proponents had previously submitted a 350-page draft to the Office of International Affairs of the National Park Service.

After input from various government agencies, the draft was approved and sent to the International Council on Monuments and Sites, the group that earlier had held its symposium in San Antonio. On January 21, 2014, the council made a full report to the World Heritage Committee. The report described the nomination as a serial nomination of five frontier missions along a twelve-kilometer stretch of the San Antonio River basin. In addition to the missions and the Alamo, it included Rancho de las Cabras near Floresville.

The missions were described as a unique complex of frontier missions and a remarkable example of Spanish colonization and evangelization. The report called the missions a persistent and vibrant testimony to an interweaving of cultures from the European and North American continents.

In fall 2014 World Heritage officials visited San Antonio. They were pleased with the restored river and the portals to the missions. We took them on a tour of the churches within the missions that had been restored. Father David Garcia, the former rector at San Fernando Cathedral, was instrumental in leading the effort to raise $15 million to restore the four churches. While rector of San Fernando Cathedral he was a leader advocating the reconstruction of Main Plaza.

The delegation was impressed with the work completed in the churches at Concepción, Mission San José, and San Juan. At Concepción, for example, the stucco walls were returned to their original condition and lighting was improved.

The church architect at Mission Concepción knew about

astronomy and geometry. At certain times of the day, sunrays stream through a window onto a painting of Mary above the altar. At the same time, another ray shines into the dome of the sanctuary, hitting the floor in the center of the cross-shaped church.

The two-story Mission San José adobe church with its bell tower dominates the northern sector of a large enclosed plaza. New lighting highlighted the mission's artwork and architectural features. The carved stone façade had been treated to remove moisture.

The Mission San Juan church, built in a narrow rectangle with eighty pews, was the smallest of the four mission churches. Its renovation cost $2.2 million.

Restoration work at Mission Espada was still under way. The convent and garden grounds were being restored. It would be completed in 2015.

While we were confident we had made a good case, we knew the effort could fail because Congress had refused to pay the nation's UNESCO dues. In the 1990s Congress had passed a law stopping payment of dues to any organization that recognized Palestine. In 2011 UNESCO recognized Palestine, and the following October the United States stopped paying dues.

We devised a strategy to convince Congress to pay only the portion of dues that provided financial support to the World Heritage Committee, which was $815,000 annually. Unfortunately, Congress did not pass the appropriation.

Throughout 2014, increasing numbers of people began to jog, ride bicycles, and walk down the river, and many came to visit the missions. During the first six months, 732,000 people visited the four missions, up from 521,705 visitors the full previous year.

In March we received the good news that the International

Council on Monuments and Sites had recommended to the World Heritage Committee that the Alamo and missions be inscribed as a World Heritage Site. This recommendation was a significant achievement: the odds of being inscribed without its approval would have been very slim.

The report to the World Heritage Committee made clear that the four missions were selected based on their geographical and functional relationship to the San Antonio River basin. Had Bexar County not restored the river, built the four portals to the missions, and created pathways along the river, I do not believe they would have been considered for inscription.

On the morning of May 26 I walked into the visitor center at Mission San José to meet a tall, lanky African American woman who would play a role in helping us with the World Heritage Committee. Crystal Nix-Hines, US ambassador to UNESCO, stood looking at books on the history of the missions.

When we were introduced, I was taken with her smile and her few, soft-spoken words. As we walked around, she took in everything, carefully studying the mission and asking questions. I gave the ambassador the two best books on the missions.

That evening as I sat by her at a dinner hosted by the city, she warmed up when I told her I was a Democrat. She was a friend of President Obama. "Make sure that members of your delegation do not lobby delegates," she warned me. "They would be offended."

"We will not," I responded. Then I explained that on the advice of the vice chairman of the National Park Foundation, John Nau, we had already turned down several lobbyists who wanted to represent us.

We organized a delegation to travel to Bonn, Germany, site of the June World Heritage Committee meeting. Principal members of our local delegation were Mayor Ivy Taylor; Rebecca Viagran, District 3 city council member; Betty Bueche, director of county facilities and parks; Snow, representing the National Park Service; Suzanne Dixon, representing the National Park Conservation Association, Sherry Dowlatshahi, the city's chief of protocol and head of international relations; Dan Naranjo, Old Spanish Missions board member; Scott, from SARA; and me.

On June 15, a few days before our delegation headed to Bonn, at a ceremonial signing at Mission San Juan, the city, county, and SARA transferred ownership of fifty-five acres to the National Park Service. The transfer required special legislation. The local congressional delegation, including Reps. Joaquin Castro, Henry Cuellar, Lloyd Doggett, Will Hurd, and Lamar Smith, introduced the bill. All of them signed a letter supporting the nomination.

Before we left for Germany, Laura Jesse, county public information officer, told me, "I want to plan a celebration in front of the Alamo at 8:30 a.m. the day after you and Mayor Taylor arrive back home. I want to order T-shirts designed by a local artist to reflect the world heritage inscription."

"Sure, plan the ceremony and order the shirts," I told her. I figured that if the Spurs could order caps and T-shirts before championship wins, so could we.

We touched down in Germany on July 1 and traveled by van from Cologne to nearby Bonn. Bonn had been the capital of West Germany until East and West Germany were reunited in 1990 and the capital moved to Berlin. The World Heritage Committee was meeting in one of the great buildings the government had left behind.

The next day the delegation gathered at the World Heritage

Committee meeting to hear several presentations for inscription, where some were rejected, some delayed, and some accepted. I was surprised to see Sebastian Lang-Lessing, conductor of the San Antonio Symphony, there. He and his wife keep an apartment in Berlin, and he had driven over to support us.

Afterward Lang-Lessing asked me, "How would you like to visit my ancestral home? Our home dates to 1865, and my cousin, William Lang-Lessing, and his family still reside there. It's located some seventy miles from Bonn in the Upper Middle Rhine Valley, an area that has been designated a World Heritage Site."

Dr. Alfonso "Chico" Chiscano, a renowned heart surgeon and Canary Island descendant, and Richard Perez, president of the Greater San Antonio Chamber of Commerce, were standing nearby, and we all said we would love to go. We arranged first to meet Taylor and some others of our delegation at Ehrenbreitstein Fortress, located on the way to Lang-Lessing's ancestral home.

As we were driving, Lang-Lessing said, "In this region, there were more than forty castles built along the Rhine. Most were constructed between the twelfth century and first half of the four-teenth century. Over time they declined and were abandoned. Only three castles were spared—Ehrenbreitstein, Marksburg, and Rheinfels."

When we got out at the Ehrenbreitstein Fortress and castle, Lang-Lessing said, "This huge fortress was first settled in the fourth millennium B.C. In about 1000 A.D., the castle was erected on the grounds."

We had lunch with Taylor and her delegation in the open plaza looking down some 360 feet to the confluence of the Moselle and Rhine Rivers. Across the rivers, we could see the town of Koblenz.

Afterward, Taylor and her group headed back to Bonn, and

Lang-Lessing drove us to Oberlahnstein, part of the city of Lahnstein. When we arrived, we pulled into a driveway leading to a large, white two-story home. William Lang-Lessing, a lawyer and a judge, greeted us in the front yard and escorted us in to meet his wife and two of their grown children. In the living room, we drank hot tea and talked about family, law, and music.

On the morning of July 5 we watched a few presentations before the World Heritage Committee before Taylor and I were called to a meeting with Nix-Hines and officials from the State and Interior Departments. They told us that our presentation was in the afternoon and that if we were inscribed, Taylor, Nix-Hines, and I each would make short speeches. State Department officials reviewed our remarks.

That afternoon we joined the twenty-one World Heritage delegates seated on the floor of convocation center. They included representatives from Algeria, Colombia, Croatia, Finland, Germany, India, Jamaica, Japan, Kazakhstan, Korea, Lebanon, and Vietnam.

We received language interpretation devices that offered up to six official languages and listened to the presentation from the International Council on Monuments and Sites and its recommendation for our inscription. We were concerned when the Portugal representative asked about a complaint from a Native American activist in San Antonio who did not support us.

When the vote was taken, we were inscribed unanimously. We gave our short speeches, and loud applause erupted across the chamber. Unlike when other inscriptions were awarded, delegates came to congratulate us personally. This was a very special moment for us as representatives of our city, state, and nation.

The Alamo and missions joined other famous places throughout the globe as World Heritage Sites. I will never forget that exciting moment. Afterward we had dinner and celebrated with our delegation.

Even after a long flight home, I woke up early on July 6 and hustled to the Alamo. People were gathering, and Jesse was passing out T-shirts that featured a drawing of Mission Concepción and, in large type, "World Heritage."

As they waited for the ceremony to begin, several hundred people stood around talking about recognition of the Alamo and the missions as among the most elite and respected sites in the world.

As master of ceremonies, I introduced Father Garcia to give an opening prayer and then Taylor to speak. She announced that the city would create a zoning ordinance to protect the Alamo and the missions from intrusive development. I said we would work with the city to clean up some of the areas around the missions and to foster economic development that would complement the missions.

Representatives of organizations that supported the effort spoke briefly, and we closed with a blessing from Native American descendants Epifanio Hernandez and Adrian Ramirez.

Three months later, on October 17, at an inscription ceremony at Mission San José, US Interior Secretary Sally Jewell unveiled a plaque commemorating the inscription. I had previously met Sally in Washington after she had succeeded Ken Salazar as interior secretary. Weekend events included a concert, art exhibit, and worship service, which was a great ending to our quest for the World Heritage designation.

# SAN PEDRO CREEK

San Pedro Creek flows through the west side of downtown, winding its way south to a junction with the San Antonio River just north of Mission Concepción. The Spanish first settled along San Pedro Creek where, in 1718, they established a presidio and Mission San Antonio de Valero. The mission later was moved and turned into a fort that is now the Alamo.

San Pedro Creek, like the river's Mission Reach, had become an unsightly drainage ditch. For many years people had advocated that the historic creek and birthplace of our city be restored. If the downtown portion could be restored, it would extend to the southern portion of the creek that flows into the river just north of Mission Concepción. A walking, jogging, and hiking path alongside the creek would give people another pathway to the Mission Reach and the Missions. It could also lead to a revival of the west side of downtown, a segment of the city that had been neglected.

Back in 2012 we began seriously thinking about restoring the creek. With the economic development success of the Museum Reach of the river, we were confident that economic development in the west side downtown area would also follow the creek. Commissioner Paul Elizondo, who grew up on the banks of the creek before it was turned into a ditch, became a champion of San Pedro Creek. County Manager David Smith was enthusiastic about the project. Again, our partner was SARA, under Scott's leadership.

So the Commissioners Court, one year before we finished the Mission Reach, commissioned a preliminary engineering survey to determine the project's feasibility. It would not be an easy undertaking, because the creek was so narrow in the downtown area.

The following year, in 2013, we received the results of the study that we commissioned. It showed that creek restoration would remove thirty-eight structures and 41.2 acres from the floodplain and would improve property values by 20 percent. The project would include four miles of trails, 60,000 feet of linear walls, and 11.5 acres of landscaping. Eight city bridges and six pedestrian bridges that crossed the creek would require improvements. After completion of the pre-engineering study, we began work on the final design for the creek.

The Commissioners Court then committed $125 million to restore the creek. We wanted the creek to be different than the downtown segment of the San Antonio River. In addition to improving water quality, revitalizing the ecosystems, and enhancing flood control, we wanted to tell the story of history of our emerging cultures through the use of color, words, murals and sculpture, and tile design. We would in effect be creating an outdoor art gallery to enliven the urban landscape with the inspiring story of San Antonio de Béjar.

On September 8, 2016, we held groundbreaking ceremonies for the San Pedro Creek Improvements Project. This groundbreaking was unlike any other: the county had commissioned an original opera celebrating the founding of San Antonio on the creek. On the football field at Fox Tech High School, located at the northern entrance to the creek, the local symphony, opera, and ballet staged the first act of the beautifully written work. Behind the stage, a large digital screen showed scenes of the creek, and the opera ended with a large display of shooting streams of water colored by lights.

In the same year as the San Pedro Creek groundbreaking, the river foundation on May 11 broke ground on Confluence Park, which lies at the intersection of the river and creek. Stretching down to the river edge, the park brings art, education, and recreation together. It includes an education pavilion, a large-scale water catchment system, and ecotype demonstration areas. The $10 million project provides a unique learning environment for everyone. The county contributed $1.7 million toward the project.

In July 2017 I took a tour along with the foundation's executive director, Robert Amerman, an architect who succeeded Estela Avery when she retired. Amerman had served five years on the board prior to becoming executive director. He was instrumental in setting the vision for the park and was responsible for the construction. On a cool Saturday morning on March 3, 2018, we gathered under the large catchment center to celebrate the opening of this one-of-kind park. Young people visiting for generations to come will experience the beauty of nature and learn the importance of preserving our environment.

On May 5, the evening of San Antonio de Béjar's three hundredth anniversary, we opened the first phase of San Pedro Creek from the tunnel inlet at Fox Tech High School to Houston Street. We were honored to have the Duke and Duchess de Béjar join us. (In 1718 Bexar County was named after the Duke de Béjar.) Following several speeches, we flipped on the creek lights and fireworks went off above an electronic vision of the May 5, 1718, night sky wrapped around the tunnel inlet. It was a grand evening.

Hundreds of citizens walked with us along the creek, led by George Cisneros's Urban-15 dancers. We paused on the wide sidewalks that allowed room for bicyclists, walkers, and joggers, and enjoyed cut stonework featuring word art by John Phillip Santos and murals by Adriana Gonzalez, Katie Pell, Alex Rubio, and

Joe Lopez. Aquatic plants, trees, shrubs, and grasses framed the walls, and nineteen tile benches designed by Michael Menchaca provided resting places. Bridge railings were designed by Diana Kersey. Thirteen interpretive signs told the history of the civilizations that settled along the creek.

On June 16 King Felipe VI and Queen Letizia of Spain visited to celebrate the city's tricentennial. They attended numerous events over two days, including the grand opening of the exhibit Designing America, Spain's Imprint in the United States. They joined Tracy and me on an exhibit tour hosted on the first floor of the courthouse. We pointed out one of the maps highlighting San Pedro Creek where the Spanish built the presidio and Mission San Antonio de Valero in 1718. We held a reception for them after the tour in the restored double-height courtroom.

The San Pedro Creek restoration was a controversial project, unlike the restoration of the Mission Reach of the river. During my reelection campaign of 2014, I was severely criticized by my Republican opponent for supporting and funding the San Pedro Creek project. All the proposed artwork along the creek led some people to conclude that, while aesthetically beautiful, it was not a justifiable expenditure of public funds.

The restoration of the creek is as much about telling the story of the confluence of our cultures over the past three hundred years as it is about water. I believe that this story cannot be told fully in just words—that visual arts will make the story come alive. I am confident that the artwork will be appreciated by many generations to come; it will help them understand where we came from and how they fit in.

I also believe that art will help attract visitors as well as private development along the creek. The twenty-three-story Frost Bank

Tower, adjacent to the creek and facing Houston Street, is already under construction. The new federal courthouse, to be located on Nueva Street next to the creek, has been funded by Congress and is in the final stages of architectural drawings. Texas Public Radio (TPR), the city, and the county have reached an agreement to restore the Alameda Theater and build office space for TPR.

I believe the connectivity of the Mission Reach, San Pedro Creek, and the World Heritage Missions will speak to generations to come of the history and assimilation of cultures that have made San Antonio a great city.

The Mission Reach has drawn people down to the river in increasing numbers. From 2015 to 2016, 5,443 paddlers rode the river; from 2014 to 2016, people biked 498,721 miles on bikes they rented from B-Cycle; and from 2012 to 2017, all told, 1,537,541 people walked, jogged, and biked along the trails along the Mission Reach.

The missions' World Heritage designation has had a huge impact on the number of visitors. According to the National Park Service, 1,356,911 visitors have come to the four missions in 2016, up from 521,705 in 2013. They spent more than $79 million in communities near the park and more than $110,688,200 cumulatively. In other words, a 2013 report to the Commissioners Court that the World Heritage designation would generate an additional $100 million proved to be true.

The Mission Reach also has spurred development along the river's southern reach. CPS Energy is converting the long-closed Mission Road Power Plant to an innovation center called EPIcenter. Located on the river next to Roosevelt Park, it will house private companies and public institutions researching alternative energy uses.

Housing projects such as the Flats at Big Tex, Agave Apartments, Southtown Flats, Cevallos Lofts, and Steel House Lofts were all built near the river. Additional housing units have been announced on the river next to the Roosevelt Golf Course and Lone Star Brewery, as well as adjacent to Mission Concepción.

While the missions are a string of pearls along the Mission Reach, this largest ecological restoration of an urban river in the country offers many other pearls as well. It has provided a home for native plants, wildlife, and fish. Generations of people will continue to come to the river to kayak, canoe, fish, hike, and bike.

The Mission Reach and the missions are inspiring citizens to celebrate our history, culture, and environment. Future generations will be responsible for preserving the river and continuing to enhance it.

I believe San Pedro Creek will also prove to be a people place. The two miles of murals, words, colors, and patterns will weave history and culture into one monumental story of our community. We will walk in the footsteps of our ancestors, giving us a sense of where we came from and how we fit in. Collectively, through many generations, we have achieved what we are today.

# TWO

# *The Symphony and the Tobin Center*

CLASSICAL MUSIC got off to a roaring start in San Antonio when the Germans came to town. They started settling in Texas in the 1830s, and by the 1850s more than one-third of San Antonio's population was German.

Both of my grandparents on my father's side were among the German immigrants. My grandfather, Adolph Wolff, and my grandmother, Emma Bonn, came with their families to Texas in the 1870s. They married in Pflugerville and then moved to San Antonio.

In 1887 German immigrant Carl Beck founded a forty-nine-piece orchestra in San Antonio. Beethoven Hall opened in 1895 and became the orchestra's home. In 1905 Carl Hahn organized a symphony orchestra.

Classical music leaped forward in 1939 when Max Reiter, a German-Italian immigrant, founded the San Antonio Symphony, an organization independent of its predecessors. By 1943 it employed seventy-five professional musicians. The symphony was one of only nineteen major orchestras in the nation, and the only one in Texas. It brought national attention to the city by hosting several world premieres by important composers. Reiter led the symphony until his death in 1950.

Victor Alessandro followed him, producing works of German composers such as Richard Wagner, Richard Strauss, Johannes Brahms, and Ludwig van Beethoven. He also produced several operas, including famous ones by Giuseppe Verdi and Giacomo Puccini. Under his leadership, the orchestra made its first major recording. He conducted the symphony for twenty-six years, until his death in 1976.

With Alessandro's passing, the San Antonio Symphony began a slow downward spiral. New kinds of music drew audiences away from classical music. Eleven years after Alessandro's death, the symphony went dark. The year was 1987, the same year I was elected to the city council.

I naturally felt a strong link to my German heritage and wanted to preserve the great music and culture it had brought to San Antonio. All great American cities understand the significance of their symphonies and stand up to support them. We needed to step up as well.

As a councilman, I teamed up with Mayor Henry Cisneros to revive the symphony. We increased city funding, and the private sector agreed to raise additional money. The symphony came back to life.

The city council also voted to purchase the 2,300-seat Majestic Theatre as a home for the symphony. Joci Straus—the mother of Joe Straus, who would become the speaker of the Texas House of Representatives—created Las Casas Foundation to restore the interior of the 1929 theater, raising $9 million for the restoration. The San Antonio Symphony opened there in 1989.

After I was elected mayor in 1991, we substantially increased the city's annual contribution to the symphony to $500,000. With a new symphony home and increased funding, Christopher Wilkins, music director, led the symphony to new heights. In 1995 it received two national awards, the ASCAP award for programming of contemporary music, and a Magic of Music grant from the John S. and James L. Knight Foundation.

I was proud of the orchestra members and considered them essential to fostering a creative class of talented citizens. They inspired future musicians through education programs they developed with school orchestras and bands. It has been well documented that students do better in academic classes when they are inspired by the arts.

Orchestra members also created and played great works of classical music, the foundation for all forms of music we hear today. One of the most famous musical transitions occurred when a classically trained musician, George Martin, produced and orchestrated the music for the Beatles, introducing a distinctive and popular new sound. The creation of new forms of music continues today.

After I was term-limited out of the mayor's office in 1995, I left feeling proud that we had taken the symphony to another level and settled it in a new home. Attendance grew as the symphony offered a choice of classical and pop series.

But not long after I left office, dark clouds began to brew in the form of a broad attack on the arts at the federal level. This attack eventually had a devastating effect on the symphony.

The National Endowment for the Arts came under a withering attack after Republicans took control of the House of Representatives and elected Newt Gingrich as house speaker. He sought to eliminate the National Endowment for the Arts and the Corporation for Public Broadcasting. They both survived, but in 1996 Congress cut funding for the endowment almost in half, from approximately $180 million to $99.5 million.

The national attack on the arts filtered down to San Antonio. In 1996 Mayor Bill Thornton, who had followed me, felt the first wave of anti-art sentiment when its leaders first took a swing at public art, the beginning of a broad attack on the arts at the local level.

On June 21, 1996, when a public arts ordinance came up for renewal, it failed by one vote. This public arts ordinance, enacted when I was mayor, required that 1 percent of every capital project be dedicated to public art. Artists bring a different perspective to a construction project in terms of decor as well as functionality. Public art comes from studios and to the streets, where all can share its emotion and beauty.

After the vote, I wrote a letter to council encouraging them to reconsider the ordinance. I wrote, "Artists are innovative and creative in the design of projects. We can look with pride to our new library and council chambers that were built, furnished, and decorated with creative ideas from artists."

After my letter generated a front-page story in the *San Antonio Express-News*, Thornton called to say he would make a renewed effort.

He ran into opposition when *Express-News* columnist Roddy Stinson criticized the proposal. Then People on Watch, led by former mayoral candidate Kay Turner, warned council members not to vote for the ordinance.

On July 18 the council reconsidered the ordinance, this time passing it 7 to 4. The council had taken the heat.

While Thornton stood up to opposition, his victory was short-lived. Councilman Howard Peak, who had voted against the art ordinance, defeated Thornton in the mayoral race the next year, setting the stage for a broader local attack against the arts.

After Peak's election, Councilman Robert Marbut led the anti-art effort. He said he would like to see the city's Department of Arts and Cultural Affairs, which had been established in 1987, die. He called it "a bastion of special interests." Marbut also moved to do away with 1 percent for public art in capital projects and to cut the city's arts budget. The arts department survived, but the council eliminated the provision of 1 percent for art for capital projects and cut the arts budget by 15 percent.

Supporters of the arts finally realized that when one segment of the arts is attacked, a broader attack will follow. They knew they would have to be more active politically.

Bill FitzGibbons, a sculptor and adjunct professor at Trinity University, organized Picasa (People Involved in Culture and Art in San Antonio). Its goal was to defend public money for the arts. "There's a culture war going on in San Antonio," he told the *New York Times*.

While the culture war was under way, I stepped back into the political picture as county judge on May 8, 2001. Before my appointment, I had supported former councilman Ed Garza for mayor. As a councilman, he had fought against the attack on the arts. He was elected mayor three days before I became county judge.

A year later, in fall 2002, Garza and I teamed up to change the perception of the arts. To be successful, we needed to position the arts as an economic driver as well as a cultural amenity. We cochaired a collaborative that brought together thousands of people over two years to learn about the significance of the arts and to develop a plan for arts expansion.

Later that year I walked into a convention center conference room to an impressive showing of more than sixty members of a steering committee to review a study conducted by consultants. After reviewing the study, the group agreed to an eighteen-month work schedule to create a plan for the arts, adjourning to join more than five hundred citizens to hear Richard Florida, the author of *The Rise of the Creative Class.* "Cultural vibrancy leads to economic development," Florida told the group. "It does not mean just museums and a symphony. It takes creative people in whatever field they represent to build a great city."

After Florida's speech, the attendees agreed to address six challenges: funding, facilities, undercapitalized nonprofit organizations, lack of communication within the cultural sector, lack of public awareness, and lack of understanding the connection between the arts and economic development.

Unfortunately, while the collaborative was under way, the symphony went dark again in 2003. It had survived huge federal and local government cuts by spending most of its endowment. When that money ran out, it not only went dark for a time but also declared bankruptcy. Reorganizing would take time.

In 2004, as work continued on the arts plan, Tracy and I decided to take a musical vacation to Vienna. We wanted to see a city that understood the significance of symphonic music—as well as other forms of music—in building a great city. Vienna, known as "the City of Music," ranks first in the world in quality-of-living surveys primarily because it is a major cultural center. It also has been ranked as most prosperous city in the world and number one as a major international destination for conventions.

The two-thousand-year-old city, located on the banks of the Danube River, is considered one of four European cultural centers for theater, opera, and classical music. With more than fifty theaters and opera houses, Vienna has been the home of famous composers including Wolfgang Amadeus Mozart, Franz Schubert, Johann Strauss, Joseph Haydn, Gustav Mahler, and Arnold Schoenberg.

We stayed at the Imperial Hotel on the great Ringstrasse, an elegant boulevard that circles the Innere Stadt, the heart of the city. Emperor Franz Joseph, Queen Elizabeth II, President John F. Kennedy, and Luciano Pavarotti had all stayed in the hotel.

One morning we stopped by Café Landtmann, where Sigmund Freud liked to smoke his cigars. We then walked over to St. Stephen's Cathedral, a Romanesque church that dates back to 1147. Mozart's unfinished dirge, his *Requiem Mass,* was performed in the church. The next day we toured the Theater an der Wien, where on December 22, 1808, Beethoven premiered his Fifth and Sixth Symphonies. That evening we went to the Konzerthaus, home of the internationally renowned Vienna Symphony, to hear Beethoven's Fifth. The following day we visited the Hofburg Imperial Palace, where Beethoven premiered three symphonies: the Seventh and Eighth and "Wellington's Victory Symphony." We then visited the Austrian National Library to view Beethoven's handwritten manuscript of the Third Symphony.

We returned home inspired by the music and culture of Vienna. We thought our city needed to make a statement in support of the performing arts by building a first-class performing arts center for the symphony and other local performing arts groups. A first-class performance hall makes clear the importance of the performing arts, much as museums and galleries do for the visual arts of paintings and sculpture.

Though the Majestic Theatre was home for the symphony, the

auditorium was too big and the acoustics were poor. The private company that ran the Majestic was more interested in booking performing groups that produced more revenue.

After we arrived home, the symphony, to our delight, emerged from bankruptcy. It restructured the board, reduced expenses, cut the size of the orchestra, and shortened the length of the season.

The following year, on January 19, 2005, the arts collaborative adopted a ninety-one-page document containing thirty-eight strategies dealing with access, economic development, community awareness, authenticity and creativity, and resources. One strategy was to build a performing arts center that I had advocated for. I began to speak out on the necessity of a new performance hall and called for a public-private initiative to build it and a nonprofit organization to operate it.

The *San Antonio Business Journal* highlighted my push on its front page in January. It quoted me as saying, "If we can build the arena and a dome, there is no reason we cannot step up and build a first-class center for the ballet, the symphony, the opera, and other performing arts." At the time I had no idea how we would accomplish the proposal, but at least I was starting to build public support. It would take another two years to develop a plan to finance the performing arts center.

Meanwhile, the collaborative helped set the stage for a revival of the arts. We used a 2002 study from Americans for the Arts to push for more public and private funding. The study found that San Antonio ranked twenty-sixth among the fifty largest cities in per capita spending for the arts. Dallas spent $11.92 per capita; Austin, $7.97; Houston, $4.33; and San Antonio, only $2.78.

With the changing perception of the arts, Garza restored public funding for the arts and revived the public arts ordinance. Felix

Padrón, director of the city's cultural arts department, became the point person in selecting some fifty public art projects.

After Phil Hardberger was elected mayor in May 2005, he led the council to increase the arts budget by 37 percent. My son Kevin, a Navy veteran of a foreign war, was elected to the city council the same year. He played an important role in advocating for the increased funding. The council action was significant in restoring the symphony to strong financial health.

As county judge, I took the lead in establishing The Fund, a nonprofit organization that has raised hundreds of thousands of dollars for the arts over the last decade. The Commissioners Court also established an arts internship for ten students to work each summer with ten arts organizations selected by The Fund.

We knew we were on the right track after a study commissioned locally found that the creative industry has a $1.2 billion economic impact on San Antonio and employs nearly twelve thousand people. The five segments of that industry include design and advertising; museums and collections; performing arts; specialized schools of music, drama, and other arts; and visual arts and photography.

The arts also were important to our large tourism industry. One study found that 81 percent of US adults who travel are considered historic/cultural travelers. They stay longer and spend more money than other tourists.

While public support for the arts grew, so did private contributions. Several major art patrons stepped forward. One was Linda Pace, who also added glamour to the arts revival by staging parties and events celebrating contemporary art. She had grown up in San Antonio and graduated from Trinity University with an art degree. Her father founded Pace Foods, best known for its Pace Picante Sauce.

Pace bought a building downtown on North Main Avenue and remodeled it to include a gallery, apartments, and art studios. She used the building to house Artpace, a nonprofit contemporary art gallery with an international artists-in-residence program. She then bought a building on Flores Street in Southtown that had housed a candy factory and then a survey company. Located a few blocks from the King William neighborhood, it became CAMPstreet Residences with twenty condominiums. Pace moved from her Terrell Hills home into a fifth-floor condo, with exhibition space on the sixth floor. She also located her studio in the building and established her foundation office nearby.

In December 2005, Tracy and I attended a party in Pace's restored building. Men in tuxedos and women in evening gowns made their way along the corridors, which were lined with works by local artists. Eventually we gathered in an open-air pavilion on the rooftop. Under the stars, we drank and danced to jazz music. From the CAMPstreet rooftop, we could see how art had transformed Southtown into a vibrant community. Abandoned buildings had been turned into apartments and studios. We saw galleries, studios, small music venues, coffeehouses, and chic bistros throughout the area.

We could see the historic King William neighborhood where German immigrants in the late nineteenth century built grand Victorian and Romanesque Revival mansions. Many of the homes, which had deteriorated after the turn of the century, had been restored.

Sandwiched into the King William neighborhood was a reminder of the German musical heritage. Beethoven Hall, a thriving German beer garden at 422 Pereida, is home to the Beethoven Maennerchor, a German choral and heritage society committed to preserving German song and classical music. We also could see the Blue Star Arts Complex facing the river at the edge of the neighborhood. It included a 12,000-square-foot contemporary art museum, as well as apartments, art studios, and commercial space.

Southtown demonstrates that artists can foster the revitalization of neighborhoods, bring housing developments, and expand commercial development. Artists who chose to live and work in the area brought life to a once-dormant area. As we danced and looked around Southtown, Tracy said, "This is San Antonio's version of the New York Truman Capote parties. I believe we have arrived."

That was a grand evening that we will never forget. Unfortunately, it was the first and last time we had a grand party with Pace on her rooftop building: she died two years later.

Her legacy continues, however. Many years later, in June 2017, I spoke at the groundbreaking ceremonies on Camp Street for a $16 million, 14,000-square-foot cast concrete building with mica aggregate and large glass windows. Known as Ruby City for its crimson finish, it will hold over eight hundred pieces of contemporary art that Pace had collected from all over the world. Sir David Adjaye, who designed the Smithsonian Institute National Museum of African American History, and Irby Hightower, whom I mentioned in the last chapter, were the architects. It will face the restored San Pedro Creek.

After Pace's party, Tracy and I were more inspired than ever to take art to another level. As the year 2006 came around, I finally found my footing toward a way to build a performing arts center.

As you will recall from this book's introduction, that's the year I began to explore using the hotel motel and car rental tax to fund the center. Two years later, in 2008, the Commissioners Court agreed to call a bond election that would contain four propositions, one of which was a new performing arts center.

Of the four propositions, I thought the cultural facilities task force had the most difficult job preparing for the election. It was charged with defining the scope of a performing arts center, setting up a nonprofit to manage it, and deciding where to build it. I appointed Tracy's close friend Debbie Montford to chair the cultural facilities task force. She also was board chair of the San Antonio Symphony and a founding member of Texas Women for the Arts. She understood the prerequisites of a state-of-the-art performance hall necessary for the symphony and other performing arts organizations.

My friend Bruce Bugg Jr. was appointed chairman of the subcommittee on finance. Bugg graduated from Southern Methodist University with a bachelor's and law degrees. I had known him since the days when I chaired Target 90, the organization former mayor Henry Cisneros had created in 1983 to set goals for the city to accomplish over a seven-year time frame. Bugg was a young lawyer at the time, just beginning his career.

He later became the lawyer for Robert L. B. Tobin. Tobin was born in San Antonio in 1934, the son of Edgar and Margaret Batts Tobin. Edgar was the founder of Tobin Aerial Mapping Company, which later became Tobin Aerial Surveys. Edgar died in a plane crash in 1954, when Robert was twenty years old. Robert joined the family firm, but his real interest was the arts. He became an art collector and patron and was passionate about the performing arts, particularly the symphony and opera. Tobin had served on the board of directors of the New York Metropolitan Opera and the Santa Fe Opera. He also gave the McNay Art Museum in San Antonio a total of one thousand theater set and costume designs. Later Linda Hardberger, director and curator of the Tobin Theater Arts Fund, would join two other authors to write *Making the Scene,* a book about scene design and the Tobin Collection.

Tobin died in 2000 and left his fortune to the Tobin Foundation. Bugg would become one of two board members and chair of the $50 million foundation. Tobin's passion for the performing arts and the appointment of Bugg as the finance chair of the task force would prove to be the key in the building of the first-class performing arts center.

Finding an appropriate site for the venue in the center of the city was critically important, and the task considered a number of options.

I called Ken Halliday, CEO of Silver Ventures, developers of the Pearl Brewery site, to see if his organization was interested. The multiuse development was under construction on the north side of downtown. He was interested and suggested we look at the Bass Performance Hall in Fort Worth. Montford and Bugg joined us on a trip to Fort Worth for a visit with Paul Beard, managing director. He gave us a tour of the $72 million performance hall, built in 1981. It was a grand hall, similar to the great opera houses of Europe. Located downtown, it had spurred economic development in the area.

Beard said while local performing arts groups had priority, the facility made its money from Broadway shows and touring artists. He said he had kept the theater in the black for the previous decade, but many years had been tight. He suggested we hire a consultant to draw up a business plan. We took his advice.

The Commissioners Court agreed to hire Bud Franks, who had managed the Hobby Center for the Performing Arts in Houston, as a consultant. We provided funding to develop a business plan and to hire a team of acoustic and audio experts and theater planning and design experts. We wanted a first-rate, flexible, intimate music hall with acoustics that would create a rich, warm vibration.

While several sites were under consideration, someone floated the idea of renovating the 4,800-seat iconic Municipal Auditorium, which had been built in 1926 as a memorial to World War I veterans killed in action. Located downtown on six acres along the San Antonio River and designed by the firm of well-known architect Atlee B. Ayres, it was recognized as one of the best examples of the Spanish Colonial Revival style. Stone ornaments were carved into the twelve-sided limestone structure, while domed towers framed the entrance.

In 1979 a fire had gutted the interior. Two years later, voters approved a $9.1 million bond issue to repair the auditorium, and the project was completed in 1985. The huge building was used for concerts and other events, including boxing matches. Because it was too large and had terrible acoustics, it was booked only eighty days a year, resulting in an annual loss to the city of more than $500,000.

Next to the auditorium was another 1926 building originally intended as a restaurant and hotel but never used for those purposes. Eventually the city fire department began using it.

The auditorium abuts the San Antonio River south of Lexington Avenue north of downtown. As the task force looked at the building, work was under way improving the river to connect the auditorium to the Pearl Brewery development. Planning experts believed that the auditorium's revival would spur development along the river some 1.5 miles to the Pearl.

Mayor Hardberger said he would consider making the auditorium available. Montford and I visited with City Manager Sheryl Sculley, and she liked the idea too. Sculley is a smart cookie who saw this as an opportunity to rid the city of a costly asset.

We toured the facility with Michael Guarino of Ford Powell & Carson Architects, who had worked on the Long Center for the Performing Arts in Austin. He said that to get the proper acoustics, it would be necessary to gut the auditorium's interior and create a roofline some forty feet higher.

By early November Halliday had decided Silver Ventures did not want the performance hall at the Pearl site. At breakfast at El Mirador about that time, Hardberger and I agreed that the auditorium not only made sense financially but also would mean one fewer facility to compete with a performing arts center. We also believed voters would appreciate seeing the city and county work together.

Hardberger agreed to take the matter to the city council, where two weeks later it voted 9–1 to make both the auditorium and the building next door available.

The cost estimate for a performing arts center exceeded the county's proposed $110 million investment by some $30 million. Bugg suggested creating a nonprofit foundation to raise additional funds and to manage the facility.

In late 2007 the Bexar County Performing Arts Center Foundation was formed; the initial directors were me, Bugg, Hardberger, Montford, and Susan Reed, who at that time was the district attorney. We appointed Bugg foundation president, and he began assembling a board and hiring an interim president.

Both buildings would be transferred to the newly created foundation. The city also agreed to provide $500,000 annually to the foundation for the first five years.

A few weeks later actor Tommy Lee Jones met with Bugg and me to suggest that we include a small theater within the complex. Jones had been nominated four times for academy awards, and won as best supporting actor in the film *The Fugitive*. He was born in San Saba and now makes his home in San Antonio. He and I shared a passion for collecting first-edition books. Tracy was a friend of Jones's wife, Dawn. They both served on the board of the Briscoe Western Art Museum, which was under construction. Jones said he would help assemble a cast of actors to perform in the theater. When we said we would support the theater idea, he invited us to see the Harvard Theater in Cambridge, Massachusetts.

The Joneses invited Tracy and me, along with Bugg and his wife, Alethea, to Cambridge to see the theater and attend the fortieth anniversary of the 1968 Harvard-Yale football game. Jones had played guard on the Harvard team that scored sixteen points in a comeback the last few minutes of the game to tie Yale—one of the classic college games of all time.

On a very cold day with temperature in the twenties, we sat on concrete seats in Harvard Stadium. My toes felt as if they would freeze off as we watched Harvard beat Yale. The following day we toured the Harvard Theater, where, backstage, Jones explained which props were necessary.

After we returned home on December 6, the task force on cultural facilities recommended that the Commissioners Court should allocate $110 million to renovate Municipal Auditorium to include a studio theater and a performance hall.

Commissioner Paul Elizondo suggested reducing the allocation to $100 million and using $10 million for two additional cultural facilities. He recommended $4 million for the Briscoe museum and $6 million to renovate the Alameda Theater. The Commissioners Court accepted his proposal. Bugg now had to raise more money from the private sector.

The campaign kickoff for the performing arts center initiative, held at the Municipal Auditorium, featured a string orchestra from Northside Independent School District. At the event, the music director told me that more than three thousand students played in string orchestras. With thirteen more school districts in San Antonio, that number would multiply. I felt more confident knowing that parents of these students would support us.

As I mentioned earlier, all four propositions won voter approval, and the performing arts center, Briscoe, and Alameda won overwhelmingly with 65 percent of the vote.

Now the hard work of building the performing arts center got under way. In January 2009 after a national search, Bugg hired a president: Rodney Smith, who had extensive experience running performing arts centers.

Tracy served on the performing arts advisory committee and as a member of the task force that selected Seattle-based LMN Architects and local Marmon Mok Architecture. Final architectural plans called for removing the roof and gutting the interior. The Spanish Colonial Revival exterior front, east, and west façades would be preserved. A metal veil would cover the upper reaches of the building, hiding the mechanical systems and the difference in the height between a 230-seat studio theater and the 1,750-seat performance hall, which included twenty-nine luxury boxes. An outside plaza, stretching to the river on the building's east side, would accommodate up to six hundred people for outside events.

Meanwhile, Bugg began to raise money. On August 20, 2008, Hardberger, Bugg, and I met with AT&T officials, and they agreed to make the first large gift, of $5 million. This would be their last large gift in San Antonio, because they were moving the company headquarters to Dallas. You might say the gift was a going-away present.

While planning and fundraising for the performance hall moved forward, Tracy agreed to serve on the San Antonio Symphony search committee for a new conductor. In February 2010, the committee selected German conductor Sebastian Lang-Lessing as the eighth music director in the symphony's seventy-year history. He had a distinguished record as conductor of the Deutsche Oper Berlin, and Orchestre Symphonique et Lyrique de Nancy.

To complement the symphony, businessman Mel Weingart and Linda Hardberger organized an opera company to perform in the center. Weingart, who earned a BSBA degree from the University of Denver, is chairman and president of the Tobin Theatre Arts Fund. Later in 2017, after Opera San Antonio had a financial shortfall, Blair Labatt became chairman and brought stability to the organization. Labatt has a PhD in English literature from the University of Virginia and a master's from Oxford. He is president of Labatt Food Service, a large local food distribution company.

The company worked with the San Antonio Symphony to provide the music. Up to the 1970s, the symphony had staged opera.

After the announcement of the newly formed opera, Bugg invited Tracy and me to Santa Fe. As a board member of the Santa Fe Opera, he wanted us to tour the facility, attend a board dinner, and go to a performance. Tracy and I were already familiar with the open-air theater a few miles from the city in an isolated pocket of the Jemez Mountains: we had attended several operas there.

In 1957 John Crosby, a conductor from New York, had led the effort to build a rustic, redwood, roofless 480-seat theater. Ten years later, a fire destroyed it. After the fire, the Santa Fe Theater was rebuilt to accommodate 1,366 people with a partial roof covering some of the seating. A dramatic roofline was added in 1997 to cover all seating but with open sides.

We toured the back rooms where costumes were made and sets built. "We will not be able to re-create this comprehensive operation back home," Bugg said. "But I wanted you and Tracy to see this so you would know how expensive and complex creating and putting on an opera can be."

"Our new opera company will need to rent sets and costumes," Tracy said.

We later attended the board dinner and met several members from across the United States. The powerful board had the financial ability to sustain the costly operation. That night we saw *Madame Butterfly*.

Back home we ran into some rough waters with the San Antonio Conservation Society and the city's Historic and Design Review Commission. The Conservation Society opposed the height of the veil, and the commission raised several design objections.

Over six months, Hardberger, Bugg, and I attended several meetings of the Historic and Design Review Commission. At each meeting, would-be architects on the committee kept making more and more recommendations for changes.

They also tried to prevent us from removing the generic name, Municipal Auditorium, from the front of the building. If they had prevailed, they would have jeopardized a gift of $15 million from the Tobin Endowment to name the building in honor of Robert Tobin.

Finally, after a six-hour meeting on March 16, 2011, the Historic and Design Review Commission approved the plans. All the delays and numerous revisions cost an additional $800,000.

We received a shock a few days later, on March 27, when the center's president, Smith, died from a heart attack. Franks, the county's consultant on the project, assumed his duties.

Because the Commissioners Court had cut $10 million from the proposed allocation to the performing arts center we decided to make up partially for the cut. In 2011 we allocated an additional $8 million for a Medal of Honor portal from the river up to the performing arts center to commemorate thirty-two Medal of Honor recipients who were born, reared, enlisted, or retired in San Antonio.

This was a particularly proper setting, given than the original auditorium had been dedicated to World War I servicemen who were killed in action. Also, two other memorials had been erected on Veterans Memorial Plaza on Auditorium Circle. One was *Hill 881 South* by sculptor Austin Deuel, dedicated in 1986 to veterans of the Vietnam War. The Korean War memorial *Night Watch* was erected next to it in 1994.

By funding the Medal of Honor portal, the county saved the Tobin Center several million dollars because it did not have to build the entrance from the river.

On May 10, 2011, interior demolition began. Less than a month later, to our surprise a lawsuit was filed asking for an injunction to stop construction of the center. The plaintiffs in the lawsuit were Sharyll Teneyuca and Placido Salazar of the American GI Forum.

Sharyll Teneyuca was in the process of writing a book about her aunt, Emma Tenayuca. In 1939 Emma Tenayuca was attending a communist rally at the Municipal Auditorium when a crowd of five thousand people attacked the auditorium, throwing bricks and rocks. She escaped from the mob, was blacklisted, and was forced to move away from San Antonio. Many years later she moved back to the city to teach. She died in 1999.

The suit alleged that the county had promised voters a new performing arts center and that partially demolishing the old building and retaining the Municipal Auditorium façade was not the same as producing a new building. Her attorney said, "It's a fraud on the voters." Many, however, thought that the lawsuit was less about the building than about publicizing Teneyuca's forthcoming book.

Hardberger and I attended a court hearing on June 28. Our lawyers showed the court that plans for the Municipal Auditorium site were discussed several times during the election and that, in fact, fraud lay with the plaintiffs. They testified that they had voted in the election when, in fact, they had not. They had perjured themselves. State District Judge Victor Negrón did not grant the injunction, ruling that the plaintiffs had no standing to file the suit. They asked for a rehearing, were denied, and appealed. After we won in the appeals court, they appealed to the Texas Supreme Court.

Even though we had won at the district and appellate levels, we faced a time problem. We had to sell additional bonds, and the lawsuit would have put a cloud over marketing the bonds. So we agreed to pay them $80,000, with the performing arts board approving the settlement on July 18, 2012. As always, the lawyers came out best. Their lawyer received $40,000, and ours took down $100,000.

One month after the settlement, we completed demolition and were ready to begin constructing the interior. The Commissioners Court issued bonds that same month.

In the meantime, Bugg and Franks disagreed on some issues. Franks eventually was replaced by David Green, former president of the San Antonio Symphony. He was our third director, but it soon all worked out.

In May 2013 the Bexar County Performing Arts Board hired Michael Fresher as president and CEO. A University of Connecticut graduate, he had been vice president of finance and controller for Madison Square Gardens and then CEO of the Bushnell Center for the Performing Arts in Hartford, Connecticut. With Fresher, we had someone with the experience and authority to run a first-class performing arts center.

With all the legal issues out of the way and a new president on board, construction moved rapidly. I took several tours of the building during construction and found hundreds of workers on the site at any given time.

While construction continued, Tracy and I went to the opening of the Briscoe Western Art Museum on October 26 with our friends John and Debbie Montford. Debbie was chair of the Briscoe board, and Tracy was a board member.

The Commissioners Court had allocated $6 million to the museum, including $4 million from the 2008 bond issue and an additional $2 million for a portal to the museum. The private sector had contributed more than $25 million.

Jack Guenther, a lawyer and businessman, and Mark Watson Jr., founder of the insurance company Titan Holdings Incorporated, were the original founders of the museum. Guenther and his wife, Valerie, were the museum's largest contributors. In addition to the large contribution from the Guenthers, they gave numerous sculptures that are positioned in front of the museum and in a large sculpture garden. Famous Texas ranching families also contributed large sums of money to the Briscoe, including Jessica Erin Elliott and her family; McLean Bowman; former governor Dolph Briscoe and his daughter Janey Briscoe Marmion; and Enrique Guerra and his son Enrique "Kiko" E. Guerra III. Fully Clingman, former president of H-E-B grocery company, made a large contribution. John Montford, a former state senator, contributed and donated a large spur collection to the museum.

The museum included nine galleries containing seven hundred pieces of art. One gallery included Santa Anna's 1852 steel and gold sword. Another contained spurs and saddles. South Texas rancher Enrique Guerra and his son, José Guerra, loaned their great collection of Spanish and Mexican colonial art and artifacts.

As the year 2014 arrived, we were fast approaching completion of the Medal of Honor portal and the performing arts center. I began spending more time observing the construction as work simultaneously progressed on both projects. Each day, the picture became sharper as workers pushed toward the finish line.

On July 3 we opened the Medal of Honor portal. Seven bronze monuments, sitting atop black granite plinths, stretched from the river up to Veterans Plaza near the Tobin Center. They were engraved with the names and stories of the thirty veterans who had earned Medals of Honor.

Two months later, on the morning of September 4, as Tracy and I approached the Tobin Center, she looked up at the gleaming metal veil rising above the restored Spanish Colonial Revival façade and said, "What a grand performance hall our community has built. This building looks as stunning as any performance hall in the world."

We walked up the steps, through the glass doors, and into the foyer. We passed the theater entrance and entered the 1,750-seat performance hall. Wraparound LED lighting separated the two levels of box seats and the third-story balcony. An array of subdued reddish colors cast by the lights gave the hall a passionate, exotic look. In front of us stood the huge stage, partially encased in an engraved-paneled orchestra shell.

We walked across a very special floor to our seats. Board member Steven Lee, president of Lee Partners, investors in real estate, came up with the idea of an adjustable floor. Bugg, with the help of his mentor Tom Frost Jr., did an incredible job raising more than $50 million in private funds enabling the addition of a $10 million floor with a hydraulics system underneath. That system could tilt the floor for performances, flatten it to stage level, or lower it below the stage for a multitiered arrangement. This gave the Tobin flexibility to hold dinners and luncheons as well as performances.

Going backstage, we joined members of the symphony as they warmed up. Lang-Lessing, music director and conductor, said to us, "What an honor it is to be the first to play in this grand hall. Thank you."

The stage had been set to accommodate the orchestra, council members, commissioners, and board members of the Bexar County Performing Arts Center. The orchestra opened with two short pieces. The oboes, horns, violins, violas, basses, flutes, clarinets, bassoons, horns, trumpets, trombones, tuba, and percussion came together to create a great sound in the acoustically perfect theater.

Tracy said, "I have never heard notes like this in the Majestic Theatre. The clarity of sound is pitch-perfect."

Next came my remarks: "I want to thank my partner and the love of my life, Tracy, who inspired me to move forward with this project. I learned that a whisper late in the evening is best remembered the next morning. Today we send a message to everyone to come and share in the richness and beauty of life through the sounds of music and the elegance of dance."

That evening, Tracy and I returned to be entertained by the city's ballet, symphony, and opera. The ballet performed scenes from *Swan Lake* and *Carmen*. Dancing in front of the orchestra, they presented a dynamic array of colors that accented the sound of music. Their emotionally expressive movements blended like a fine-tuned instrument with the music. A beautiful and saucy soprano and mezzo-soprano sang pieces from *Carmen* and *West Side Story*. The orchestra performed George Gershwin's *An American in Paris*. Then all the performers gathered on the stage to conclude with "Our Love Is Here to Stay."

Tracy and I sat in the center orchestra section holding hands and listening to the sounds of music filling the hall. The symphonic works connected us to each other through the universal language of love. The fluid bodies of the ballet dancers following the rhythm of music were like lovers seeking each other out and connecting in an embrace.

The Tobin Center for the Performing Arts Center helped spark a cultural renaissance in San Antonio. Besides the new Briscoe Western Art Museum, the Alameda Theater on Houston Street west of Main Avenue has undergone the first stages of a proposed $30 million renovation.

Other cultural institutions either have been built or expanded.

Less than a mile away from the performing arts center is the DoSeum, a 65,000-square-foot children's museum that opened on June 1, 2015. CEO Vanessa Lacoss Hurd was the inspirational leader who had envisioned the museum. Local businessman Charles Butt, chairman of H-E-B, donated more than $20 million to the museum, and the county contributed $1 million. A few blocks north of the DoSeum, the Witte Museum, the city's venerable natural history museum, has undergone a $100 million expansion, led by its president and CEO, Marise McDermott. The county contributed $3.5 million for a river habitat on the grounds, linked to the San Antonio River, which flows through Brackenridge Park behind the museum. The Witte now is ranked in the top tier of museums in the nation.

On New Braunfels Avenue, in proximity to the other two museums, the San Antonio Botanical Gardens, with a conservatory, nature trail, and extensive landscaping, has been expanded by eight acres. It offers programs and services featuring freshly grown foods, an outdoor kitchen, and a culinary garden. The county contributed $250,000.

On Jones Street, a few blocks from the performing arts center, the San Antonio Museum of Art has undergone a major expansion. It welcomes visitors from the San Antonio River with a river landing, a shaded pavilion, esplanade, and terrace. Executive Director Katherine Luber is leading the effort to acquire more land along Jones Street for a future expansion.

In June 2016 VIA, the local public transit authority, initiated a culture route connecting the four World Heritage missions and the Alamo to the other cultural institutions. Two months later I teamed up with Texas A&M San Antonio's president, Cynthia Teniente-Matson, to house more than thirty-nine thousand documents and artifacts belonging to the Daughters of the Republic of Texas after the state removed them from the Alamo Library. The Commissioners Court agreed to lease nine thousand square feet of exhibit space, office space, and two climate-controlled vaults in the former Federal Reserve building that we had purchased. The university would curate and exhibit the artifacts. County Clerk Gerry Rickhoff moved and will curate all the county historical documents to the building. District Clerk Donna Kay McKinney also will locate some of the district clerk's historic documents there.

While the arts were expanding in San Antonio, many resident performing art groups were finding their home at the Tobin to their liking. Ballet San Antonio under new leadership has put on some great performances. Tobin Board member Susan Franklin, who once was a ballet dancer in New York, was a great supporter of the ballet performing at the Tobin.

Opera San Antonio staged successful productions of *Madame Butterfly* and *Salome* in 2015. Fully staged productions of *Carmen* and *The Barber of Seville* were staged in the 2016–17 season.

Several other performing arts groups are residents, including the Youth Orchestra of San Antonio, the Children's Chorus of San Antonio, the Chamber Orchestra of San Antonio, the San Antonio Chamber Choir, and the SOLI Chamber Ensemble.

In its first year of operation, the Tobin presented seventy-three student/family events. More than thirty-seven thousand students attended free of charge. At one of the events I spoke to them about the importance of classical music and the inspiration and enrichment it could bring to their lives. The children who packed the main floor enjoyed the performance of a world-class orchestra.

While numerous musical events have been held in the center,

the San Antonio Symphony is by far the most important. The symphony gives over one hundred performances a year, including thirty-two classics, sixteen pops, fifteen operas and ballets, and several joint performances with youth orchestras. They have evolved into a first-class orchestra under the leadership of Sebastian Lang-Lessing.

Lang-Lessing emailed me about the hall in August 2016: "The San Antonio Symphony now has a home that can compete with the best halls worldwide. The symphony is developing a 'sound identity' that blends with the warm and lush colors of the hall and allows us to discover new nuances in our music making. The Tobin Center makes the city a cultural destination with national and international recognition."

In its first year at the Tobin, the symphony increased its revenue by some 20 percent. But all was not well. Previously, while Debbie Montford and then Denny Ware had been its chairs, the symphony, with an established budget of some $6-plus million, sustained itself. But going into the Tobin, its new leadership had been overly optimistic and entered into a contract with the orchestra that raised its cost to some $8 million. Symphony leaders were not able to raise sufficient funds.

In fall 2015, David Kinder, board chair; Jim Lowe, board member; and David Gross, president, came to see me about their problems. I arranged a meeting for them with three key supporters of the symphony. Soon we all met with Bruce Bugg, chairman of the Tobin Foundation; Tullos Wells, managing director of the Kronkosky Foundation; Dya Campos, H-E-B's director of government and public affairs; and Lori Houston, Center City development and operations director.

We reached an agreement of support, and in spring 2016 we

signed an agreement with the symphony to advance them funds on the condition that they would get their finances in order. Six months later they were in trouble again.

Because of the continuing problems and lack of support from funders, Dr. Alice Viroslav, a senior member of the American Society of Neuroradiology, and chairman of the Symphony Society of San Antonio, worked with Bugg, Campos, and Wells to create the nonprofit organization Symphonic Music for San Antonio. Bugg would become chairman, Campos would become president, and Wells would be vice president and secretary-treasurer. The board would be made up of major contributors.

Although the 2017–18 season got off to a good start, it soon came crashing down: in January 2018 the new board, Symphonic Music for San Antonio, pulled its support because of an unanticipated shortfall in funding for the musician pension plan.

The former board, Symphony Society of San Antonio, reconstituted itself and elected Kathleen Vale as chairperson. Vale has a BA from the University of the Americas, in Mexico City. She is a past president of the Choral Society and is the CEO of Hope Medical Supply. She hit the ground running, securing $700,000 in donations and reaching an agreement with the orchestra to continue the season. She worked with Mayor Ron Nirenberg and me to secure public funding of $718,000, to be matched by private donations. The season will be completed, but then the board must address the hard task of securing funding for the next year.

The symphony will have to take steps to broaden its appeal by creating diversified performances such as the one in September 2016. The San Antonio Mastersingers, a 120-voice chorus of volunteers under the direction of conductor John Silantien, appeared with the symphony along with two opera singers and the Children's Chorus of San Antonio to perform *Carmina Burana*, divided into three sections, "In Spring," "The Tavern," and "Court of Love." Tracy and I thought it was an incredible performance.

Another example was when the Commissioners Court commissioned an original opera to be performed outside for the groundbreaking ceremonies for the San Pedro Creek Improvements Project. On the football field at Fox Tech High School, the symphony, along with the opera and ballet, highlighted the evening.

While the symphony is reconstituting itself, the Tobin Center has already been a financial and artistic success. Under the leadership of Fresher, it staged 453 performances, with 245,000 people attending the first year. Board member William Moll, a veteran of fifty-eight years in broadcasting, provided leadership in promoting the Tobin. Aaron Zimmerman did a great job in selecting and booking the talent that performed in Tobin.

In 2016 *Pollstar*, a trade publication covering the worldwide concert industry, ranked the Tobin the number one theater in the world with two thousand or fewer seats. In July 2016 the Tobin received the Venue Excellence Award from the International Association of Venue Managers.

On December 5, 2016, we took another step to strengthen the Tobin: we held a groundbreaking ceremony for the Tobin parking garage, developed under the leadership of board members Hardberger and Tom Stephenson. Located on the corner of Fourth and Taylor Streets, one block away from the Tobin, it will provide secure parking for Tobin patrons. The city and county contributed $5 million each, and the Tobin, $7 million.

Bugg decided not to stand for reelection as chair for 2017. He had accepted an appointment to the board of the Texas Department of Transportation, the state's most powerful agency. The board selected Sam Dawson, a partner in his family's engineering business, to become chairman in 2017.

A late donation of $5 million from board member Susan Naylor in memory of her son pushed the amount raised by Bugg to more than $58 million. He led the effort to build the Tobin Center, kept it within budget, and hired a top-notch staff to run it. I do not believe another person in San Antonio could have come close to doing the job that Bugg did for the Tobin.

The versatile, world-class performing arts center on the banks of the San Antonio River is a magnet for downtown revitalization. Thousands of housing units have been built in the vicinity.

We may never be a Vienna, but San Antonio can take great pride in its cultural and arts institutions. Its booming economy can be attributed in part to the city's cultural renaissance. The Tobin Center for the Performing Arts stands at the apex.

......................................

# THREE

# The Sky Tower Hospital

A FEW MONTHS after Tracy and I were married on January 1, 1989, we bought a home on Rock Road next to the historic Oak Hills Country Club. We lived there for some twenty years, during my second term on the city council, my two terms as mayor, and my first years as Bexar County judge.

We liked living next to the golf course. Although neither of us played golf and we were not members of the club, we saw it as a private bucolic oasis once the golfers departed. I would jog the course around 6:30 a.m., and then Tracy and I would walk it in the evening hours.

Coming off the high ground of the fourteenth hole, we had a great view of the sprawling nine-hundred-acre South Texas Medical Center. The University of Texas Health Science Center and the Bexar County Hospital were linchpins of the huge number of medical buildings. They reminded me of the small role I had played in the medical center's early development.

In 1970, two years after the medical school and county hospital were built, I was elected to the Texas House of Representatives. I was the only freshman on the powerful House Appropriations

Committee, where I focused my attention on securing additional funding for the new medical school. I also included in the budget an extra $1 million for the Family Practice Center, a privilege I had as a member of the Appropriations Committee. Today that privilege has succumbed to reform.

Two years later, in 1972, I was elected to the Texas Senate. As vice chairman of the Senate Finance Committee, I played a role in expanding the UT Health Science Center. The Dental School, School of Nursing, Graduate School of Biomedical Sciences, and School of Allied Health Sciences were all created while I served in the Texas legislature.

I had the opportunity to work with several pioneers of the San Antonio Medical Foundation who played key roles in the medical center's development, including Dr. James Hollers, a dentist and president of the Medical Foundation; Dr. Merton Minter, a local physician and former member of the University of Texas Board of Regents; and Dr. John Smith Jr., a local surgeon. All have since passed away. Hollers passed in 1976, Minter in 1977, and Smith in 2003.

While I was proud of the role I had played in the expansion of the Health Science Center, I was not familiar with the working partnership between the center and the Bexar County Hospital District. On my golf course runs, I had paid little attention to a building next to the Health Science Center: Bexar County's hospital, dba University Hospital. But when word began to spread that I might become county judge, I began to take notice of it on my daily jogs and decided to do some research.

The county hospital is a Level 1 Trauma Center, providing comprehensive care for twenty-two counties and serving more than 2 million people in a geographical area larger than seventeen states. It is also the teaching hospital for the University of Texas Health Science Center.

Because the county hospital is the Health Science Center's teaching hospital, the affiliation agreement specifies that only doctors associated with the UT Health Science Center can practice in the county hospital. Seven hundred resident physicians in fifty-one accredited medical training programs rotate through the hospital. More than 1,800 medical, allied health, and nursing students train there.

I knew that if I became county judge, I would be responsible for a large part of the success or failure of the hospital system. The Commissioners Court appoints the seven-member Bexar County Hospital Board of Managers, which oversees the hospital system. Of the seven-member board of managers, the county judge appoints three, while the four commissioners each appoint one. The Commissioners Court also sets the budget and tax rate for the hospital district.

As word spread that I might be appointed county judge, one of the first people to call on me was the hospital district's board chairman, Dr. Robert Jimenez. He graduated from UT Medical Branch-Galveston and completed his residency at Boston Medical Center's Division of Psychiatry. He is a jolly, short, rotund man with considerable brain power, passion, and energy. He brought with him the hospital's president, Jeff Turner, and other top hospital executives.

We met at Sun Harvest Farms on Callaghan Road in the small office from which I had run our nine-store chain of natural food supermarkets. We had sold our business some six months earlier, and I had stayed as a consultant.

Jimenez walked in, smiled, and said, "My, what a small office.

We can barely fit in here." I laughed and said, "We try to make our offices as uncomfortable as we can so that our team will stay in the stores where our customers are. Not a bad idea for government officials."

Jimenez asked how familiar I was with the hospital district.

"Somewhat," I replied. "I do know from personal experience how important your trauma services are. One day in 1980 I arrived home to find our babysitter screaming that my two-year-old son Matthew could barely breathe. He had climbed up on the kitchen counter, grabbed some peanuts, and stuffed them in his mouth. Two of them stuck, one in each bronchial tube. When the ambulance arrived, I rode with my son to the county hospital.

"The prompt attention by an emergency team of surgeons dislodged the peanuts so he could breathe. But parts of one peanut became lodged in his lung and caused an infection.

"I spent almost a month at the hospital with my son. Two different operations were unsuccessful in extracting the peanut pieces. Infections and a high fever persisted. On the third operation, Dr. Fred Grover spent five hours in the operating room and finally removed the remnants of the peanut. Almost immediately Matthew's fever and infection disappeared.

"Matthew's life was saved first by the emergency team and then through the dedicated persistence of Dr. Grover. Matthew had excellent care all through his stay in the hospital. By the way, his unique case was also written up in medical journals."

"I am delighted that you received great service," Jimenez said. "Outside of the two military hospitals, we are still the only Level 1 Trauma Center in this part of the state. It does a great job."

I continued, "After the incident with my son, my friend Albert Bustamante, who was a county judge, asked me if I was interested in being on the board of managers. I told him that I knew Dr. Bill Thornton wanted the appointment and that he was better qualified. Albert appointed him, and he did a great job. As you know, Bill followed me as mayor of San Antonio."

Jimenez got to the heart of the visit. "We will have operational losses of $21 million for this fiscal year," he said. "If things continue going the way they are, there will be larger deficits in the out years. We also have $178 million in capital needs that have been deferred. We will need leadership and help from you."

"Give me all the information you can," I said, "and I'll study it. I will be ready to tackle the problem if the court appoints me."

I was familiar with the current operation of the hospital district, but I had a sketchy understanding of its history. When I read up, I learned a valuable lesson that would play a pivotal role in a major decision I eventually had to make.

## A TURBULENT HISTORY

In 1917 a city-county charity hospital, named the Robert B. Green Memorial Hospital after a former county judge and state senator, opened at the corner of North Leona and Morales Streets on the near west side of downtown. The city's only other hospitals were Santa Rosa Hospital, opened in 1869, and Baptist Hospital, opened in 1903.

In the 1920s the Green, as it became known, was overwhelmed with the arrival of immigrants from Mexico who had fled the Mexican Revolution and settled on the West Side near the hospital. Dr. Albert Hartman Jr., chief of surgery, recruited school interns and residents from across the nation to work at the overloaded hospital.

Legislation passed in 1930 authorized a ten-cent hospital property tax to help support the hospital's operation. While the tax support helped, the hospital struggled to continue operating throughout the next two decades.

Finally, on June 28, 1955, 72 percent of voters authorized government officials to establish the Bexar County Hospital District. The next day County Judge Charles Anderson led the Commissioners Court to approve the hospital district's creation. With one political entity in charge, responsibility and continuity could be established.

Four years after the hospital district was created, the Texas legislature approved a bill directing the University of Texas to establish a medical school within Bexar County. As a condition, the legislature required the county to build a teaching hospital within one mile of the medical school.

Many people assumed that the proposed medical school would be located downtown next to the Green. The Bexar County Hospital District was then chaired by Robert L. B. Tobin. He became chair in 1958 when he was twenty-five and was a strong advocate of locating the medical school downtown next to the Green. He was also a strong advocate for the poor, many of whom lived on the West Side near the Robert B. Green Hospital.

The newly created San Antonio Medical Foundation, founded in 1947, had other ideas. It had accepted an offer of twenty-seven acres close to the Oak Hills golf course from a partnership led by S. E. McCreless and Edgar Von Scheele. The partnership also offered to give the medical foundation another 170 acres if a medical school were established on the site. The foundation, under the leadership of Hollers and Smith, appointed a committee of one hundred citizens to decide where to locate the medical school and county hospital. Although the committee included downtown advocates, they were outnumbered.

The committee recommended building a three-hundred-bed county teaching hospital next to the proposed medical school on the Oak Hills site. It also recommended funding changes to the Green: its improvement and conversion to a clinic and outpatient facility. On May 11, 1960, the medical foundation board approved the report.

But downtown advocates did not give up. W. W. McAllister, president of the Downtown Merchants and Property Owners Association and soon to be mayor, joined Archbishop Robert Lucey; Walter Corrigan, chairman of the San Antonio Chamber of Commerce; and H. B. Zachry, construction industry leader, in advocating for the downtown location. Zachry offered two $500,000 cashier's checks to be used to obtain additional land that would be needed next to the county hospital.

But the old guard lost this battle to powerful new businessmen who wanted the hospital on the North Side and who persuaded the Commissioners Court to call a bond election on January 31, 1961. By a margin of 7–1, voters approved $5 million for the construction of a teaching hospital at the Oak Hills site and $1.5 million to convert the Green into an outpatient facility.

On February 18, 1961, Dr. Minter, chairman of the UT Board of Regents, convinced the board to accept the medical foundation's offer of one hundred acres of land in the Oak Hills area. The regents also confirmed that Bexar County had met the standards for a medical school by approving bonds for the teaching hospital. On July 21 the medical foundation transferred one hundred acres of land to the University of Texas.

Robert L. B. Tobin became a casualty of the battle when the Commissioners Court did not reappoint him in 1961. His attorney and fellow board member Jesse Oppenheimer accused the

*San Antonio Express* of printing slanderous and libelous articles against the Hospital Board, and particularly against Tobin. Some believe that because of this battle Tobin became disenchanted with San Antonio and began to spend most his time away from the city. He became a board member of the Santa Fe Opera and the New York Metropolitan Opera and donated large sums of money to them. This is the same Robert Tobin who some forty years later left a $50 million endowment for the arts when he died on April 26, 2000.

With the location settled and county bonds approved, everything appeared to be a go. But while construction funds were in place for the hospital, Bexar County commissioners did not have the taxing authority to raise enough funds to cover the hospital's $16 million annual operating budget. The burden fell on newly elected county judge Blair "Bruzzie" Reeves to find an answer. After being wounded on Okinawa during World War II, Reeves was confined to a wheelchair for the rest of his life, but that did not stop him from entering the tough world of politics.

Elected Bexar County judge in 1966, he immediately faced the unpopular task of doubling the hospital tax. He persuaded the Commissioners Court to call an election on January 17, 1967, to approve the funds. But when voters turned down the proposed tax increase, the county found itself in a fine mess.

UT regents chairman Frank Erwin and regent John Peace, a prominent local attorney, told Reeves that if the Commissioners Court could not provide the operating funds, they would convert the medical school building under construction into a nursing or dental school. Reeves quickly sought legislation to allow the Commissioners Court to double the tax rate without a popular vote. The legislation passed.

But now came the hard part: He had to convince the court to double the tax. For commissioners to overturn a recent public vote against a tax increase was unheard-of. A public outcry against the tax increase brought tremendous pressure on the court.

On July 14 the historic vote by commissioners took place just six months after voters had rejected the tax increase. Albert Peña voted no, followed by a yes from Ollie Wurzbach. Jim Helland voted yes, with A. J. Plough adding a no. Reeves cast the deciding yes vote for a 3–2 victory.

Because of four-year terms, opposition died down before Reeves stood for reelection, and he was returned to office. He would become recognized as the savior of the medical school.

In 1968 the medical school and the 504-bed Bexar County Hospital opened. The Green began phasing out inpatient services, replaced by a facility for outpatient services, including a family practice center.

The decision to build the South Texas Medical Center was enormously important in determining how the city would grow. The new center became an economic engine that drove San Antonio north, creating wealth and prosperity in its wake and leaving the inner city struggling.

Over the years numerous other medical institutions located in the South Texas Medical Center. By 2013 the various institutions had a combined budget of $3.93 billion. The center had a total employment of fifty-eight thousand, of which half were medically related. The annual economic impact was $5.4 billion.

If the medical school had been located downtown by the Green, we would have a very different city now. It would have spurred inner-city, high-density growth. We would not have the economic segregation we see today, with the vast amount of wealth located on the city's North Side.

Now that I had read about the hospital's history, I had a good understanding of the difficulty of funding the operations of the district. I also understood the issues I would face regarding any hospital expansion including taxes that would have to be levied to pay for. The Commissioners Court's action to overturn a popular vote in order to fund the hospital was the valuable lesson that would stick with me.

## THE HEALTH CARE SUMMIT

After being appointed county judge in May 2001 on a 5–0 bipartisan vote, I wasted no time addressing concerns of the Bexar County Hospital District, as I had promised Jimenez. Soon after taking office, I convened a Health Care Summit, asking my friend Bill Thornton to cochair the effort.

As I mentioned earlier, Thornton had successfully chaired the hospital board during the 1980s. By the end of his ten-year term, more than 40 percent of revenue generated by the hospital came from paying patients, which helped offset the cost of providing services to the uninsured.

After Thornton's tenure as chairman, the board approved branding the Bexar County Hospital District as University Health System. The board hoped to better identify itself with its academic partner, the Health Science Center, and enhance its image as a major teaching hospital. It may have been a good idea for public perception, but many people believe incorrectly that University Hospital is owned by the University of Texas Health Science Center.

During the summer of 2001, Thornton and I brought about twenty key health care leaders together to seek answers to industrywide issues. They identified five major areas of concern: hospital finances, workforce development, preventive health care, mental health, and trauma care. They prepared research papers and recommendations for each area.

On September 10, 2001, we convened the Health Care Summit, attended by approximately four hundred people. Attendees broke into five separate groups, each with a moderator and research and position papers we had prepared over the summer. They debated the issues and modified the papers. Group leaders reported their findings and recommendations to the main body, which voted to accept their reports. We then appointed a commission to implement recommendations.

One day after the summit, on September 11, terrorists attacked the nation. Although we became consumed with preparing the city for possible terrorist attack, we also began implementing recommendations from the summit.

Over the next two years, we made intensive efforts to enact the plan. The hospital board was successful in getting the state to implement a Medicaid upper payment limit program. This supplemental Medicaid program brought several million additional health care dollars to San Antonio, including $35 million annually for the hospital district. We also successfully lobbied for the Children's Health Insurance Program (CHIP) to be increased by 32 percent.

We worked with the Alamo Colleges Board of Trustees to implement additional nurse training programs. Thornton and Jim Reed, president of the medical foundation, raised $1.8 million for nursing scholarships. The funding enabled 654 more registered nurses to graduate from 2002 to 2006.

We worked with Mayor Ed Garza to create the Mayor's Fitness Council to promote exercise and healthy eating. Together we held numerous exercise events.

The Center for Health Care Services worked to implement many recommendations on mental health issues, including diverting people with mental health problems who had been arrested to treatment rather than jail.

While the Health Care Summit addressed the immediate funding concerns of the hospital district, I also learned a great deal from other health care providers about how to address a range of health care problems.

While working on industrywide issues I also began addressing University Hospital issues. Knowing I needed to appoint someone with financial and management experience to the board, I persuaded Alex Briseño, who had been city manager while I was mayor, to accept the appointment. He also had served as the city's finance director.

I laid the groundwork for support among commissioners to keep the hospital tax rate at its current level and take advantage of increased valuations instead of lowering the tax rate each year as we did for other county operations. We also exempted the hospital district from any tax incentives that we gave to businesses and from participating in tax increment districts.

At the same, I pushed the hospital board to tighten up its operation and seek additional revenue opportunities. The hospital board worked to qualify uninsured patients for eligible benefits that brought them additional revenue.

I also persuaded the board to stop giving $3 million a year

to Brooke Army Medical Center and Wilford Hall Hospital to treat trauma patients. While the military hospitals provided this valuable service, it also was critical to their teaching programs for military interns. Instead of giving cash, the district helped them with in-kind services.

All these measures enabled the hospital district to establish a solid financial foundation for future growth. Within two years, the district was in the black and was able to fill all nursing vacancies, raise pay scales, and purchase equipment.

During the Health Care Summit, I got to know Dr. Francisco Cigarroa, president of the UT Health Science Center, and other of its leaders. This helped me learn how important, yet tenuous, the hospital district's relationship was with the Health Science Center. Because the doctors affiliated with the Health Science Center were the only ones allowed to practice at University Hospital, there was ongoing tension about reimbursement rates, work ethic, services, cost, and an array of other issues.

Trust and respect are necessary for a successful partnership, and when trust is broken, it is hard to repair. During the summit preparation, the hospital's president, Turner, told me he had discovered that Health Science Center officials secretly had been planning to build an outpatient facility that would compete with the hospital district. He told me he wanted to send a letter threatening to stop payments to the physicians and open the hospital to private-sector doctors. I told him I was okay with sending it.

After receiving the letter, Cigarroa called me. "We were not going to move forward with the proposed facility until we talked with President Turner and the board," he said.

"You should have told them before they found out through other means," I replied.

"Well, I think Turner overreacted."

"Maybe," I said. "But tension is good. Maybe a better respect will come out of this."

"I play a violin, and when tension gets too high the strings break."

"We will not let them break," I assured him.

Later the two presidents patched things up. Cigarroa said the Health Science Center would drop its plan to build an ambulatory clinic and would always keep the hospital district informed about its plans in the future.

In my first two years as county judge, I gained a great deal of knowledge about all the issues affecting the hospital district. Most important was the need for new state-of-the-art facilities and equipment. Because of outdated buildings and equipment, the UT doctors were taking their profitable paying patients to other hospitals.

For example, we lost several elective surgeries because operating rooms were not available. Pediatric practices had moved to Santa Rosa Hospital. In 1999 University Hospital had been home to thirty-one general pediatric service lines. By the time I took office two years later, almost all the pediatric practices had been transferred to Santa Rosa, resulting in a huge financial loss to the county hospital.

At the same time, the hospital's emergency center was handling twice as many patients as it had been built to accommodate. Overcrowded conditions caused long waits, and they were projected to get worse. Wilford Hall's Level 1 Trauma Center was scheduled to close soon, which would result in more trauma cases at the county hospital.

With the financials solved, I thought it was time to move ahead with capital investments. But I had difficulty persuading Turner and the board to act. Building facilities for the future would require a great deal of capital, and many board members did not want to finance the project. But the district did not have the cash to pay for it, so expansion was stymied.

The board wanted to wait until it could accumulate enough cash to pay for an expansion, but that plan ignored escalating construction costs and a continuing loss of business.

After Turner retired in 2004, George Hernandez succeeded him and the operation gained momentum. Hernandez, an attorney and native of San Antonio's South Side, had been with the district for several years and understood the need to upgrade the facilities.

Hospital district consultants identified a shortage of intensive care unit beds, insufficient operating rooms, and a significantly undersized emergency department. The downtown Robert B. Green facility lacked state-of-the-art imaging capabilities. A modest plan was proposed to build a sixty-room addition to University Hospital and expanded clinics at the Robert B. Green downtown.

I was not impressed because the plan did not address long-term needs. I suggested to Hernandez that he take a comprehensive approach and build for the future, promising that I would help find the necessary resources. In 2006 the board authorized a study of existing facilities, asking what it would take to build a state-of-the-art hospital to exceed any other local hospital.

The resulting plan, completed in 2008, called for a 1-million-square-foot trauma tower, connecting to the hospital's existing buildings. This would take bed capacity from 488 to 721 and expand emergency facilities from forty-four bays to sixty-five. Diagnostic and treatment areas would be expanded, and a three-thousand-space parking garage would be built.

The master facility plan also called for a downtown building for ambulatory clinics, pharmacy, imaging and diagnostic facilities, an acute care and crisis care center, and additional parking. The cost for both projects was estimated at $899.4 million, with $780 million funded by debt.

This would be, by far, the largest vertical construction project, private or public, in San Antonio. The board finally realized that it had to issue debt. Unbeknownst to me, it hired a polling firm to see if there was public support for financing the plan. In June 2008 board members Briseño and Ira Smith, along with Hernandez and his team, met with commissioner Elizondo and me to reveal the poll findings. We plugged in their polling firm on a conference call.

The poll found that 53 percent of voters said they would oppose a $500 million bond issue. The firm did not poll on the $780 million necessary to finance the plan. It also did not mention the necessity of a tax increase.

The consultants told us they thought that we could turn public opinion around in the five months before a proposed November election. Briseño and Smith pressed hard for us to call the election.

I thought they were all smoking something. If the poll showed that a $500 million bond election would lose, there was no chance that $780 million would win, especially with a tax increase.

By the time everyone had his say, I was pretty heated up. "The election is a death trap," I said. "We will lose, and the new hospital will never be built. As you know, I just came off a successful bond election in May where voters had approved a $414 million venue bond issue. It took us two years to organize the campaign and raise more than $1 million for the campaign.

"There is no way that we can turn these negative numbers around in five months. I have said numerous times I would rather face the political heat in voting to raise taxes and issue the debt rather than call an election and lose. I am not going to put myself in the position that Judge Reeves found himself in when he lost an election and then had to vote to overturn the election result. I am not calling an election."

Elizondo said, "I supported you on the successful venue bond election. I need your support now."

I said, "We have the power to act without going to a vote. We just have to have the guts to do so. Paul, if you and I are together on this, we can get it done."

Briseño asked, "Don't you think there will a lot of public opposition to your proposed action?"

"Well, yes," I answered, "but why are we in office if we are not willing to stand up to public heat and do the right thing? If Paul sticks with me, we will get a court majority."

"Let's give it a try," Elizondo said.

As I stood to leave, I told Hernandez, "Let me know if you want to proceed."

One month later, on July 3, Hernandez secured approval of the board in a 5–1 vote to ask the Commissioners Court to approve the sale of $780 million in bonds and raise taxes. The plan would require an increase of 1.87 cents per $100 valuation, an average of $34.35 annually for taxpayers. The board also agreed to commit $120 million in reserves and reduce the maintenance and operation tax rate by 1.3 cents over two years.

I had already started working on court members for support

before the hospital board voted. Two commissioners said they were open to possible support.

Four days after the board's vote, Elizondo and I brought Hernandez and his team to meet with the *Express-News* editorial board. I had already talked to Bruce Davidson, editorial page editor, about the plan. He seemed receptive.

At this editorial board meeting, Hernandez explained the building plan. "Our medical emergency patients are on diversion 75 percent of the time," he said. "The UT Health Science Center is very unhappy with our outdated hospital, and its doctors are taking a lot of their patients elsewhere. If we continue to delay, we will become hopelessly behind. Also, delays in starting construction will cost us $100,000 a day."

After Hernandez and his team answered questions, I told everyone why I wanted to take action without submitting the proposal for a public vote. "We are not required by law to go to a public vote," I said. "The Commissioners Court has the right and the responsibility to act decisively just as the Commissioners Court did in 1967 after losing the public vote. We are at a turning point, and if we do not act, our hospital district will slide into a downward spiral."

"Do you think the Commissioners Court can stand up to the heat?" Davidson asked.

"I believe so. Citizens who oppose our action have the right to collect 5 percent of registered voter signatures and force an election to overturn our decision. They also can recall us."

I thought our team had performed well and answered all questions. We would have to wait to see what position the newspaper would take.

The next day, on July 8, the Commissioners Court faced its

most important decision since the building of the 1968 Bexar County Hospital. Commissioners would vote on publishing notice of our intent to sell the first phase of bonds in the amount of $274 million. At future meetings, we would vote on two more bond sales in amounts of $274 million and $213 million. We also had to approve a 1.9-cent tax increase per $100 valuation. An additional tax boost of one-half cent would be necessary in 2011.

Hernandez testified before the court that the project would include $629 million for the new hospital, $92 million for the new downtown facilities to include an urgent care center, and $178 million for renovations of existing structures for a total of $899 million.

Dr. Ronald Stewart, medical director of trauma, testified that the hospital had to turn away emergency patients 75 percent of the time. Bob Martin, president of the Homeowner Taxpayer Association of Bexar County, testified against the project. He said the right to vote should not be sacrificed on the altar of political expediency.

In closing arguments, I said that voters elected us to make hard decisions and act in the best interest of the community. Citizens had a right to overrule us by collecting signatures to call an election. I concluded by calling for us to do what was right for the long run.

The clerk called the roll. Commissioners Elizondo, Tommy Adkisson, and Sergio Rodriguez voted yes. Commissioner Lyle Larson, although he agreed with the need for the project, voted no. I voted yes.

A jubilant moment followed the strong 4–1 vote. We knew we faced subsequent votes, and opposition would grow. But we had made the right decision for the long run.

The day after our vote, the *Express-News* ran a strong statement in support of our action. "The planned expansion and renovation of the University Health System is essential.... The situation urgent, the Commissioners Court decision should stand. The expansion is unquestionably needed. No matter what happens these leaders deserve credit for showing courage in their efforts to move the county in the right direction."

The editorial was extremely important because a series of votes still lay ahead of us. If the editorial board had not supported us, we might have lost support on the subsequent votes.

On July 22, we approved the preliminary official notice to the public. We followed up with an order in August voting to approve issuance of the bonds and to levy ad valorem taxes to pay for them. On September 9, we voted to approve the overall tax rate.

This series of four court actions occurred over a two-month time frame, giving citizens ample opportunity to voice their opinions. While we had our share of criticism, the anger was not strong enough to launch a petition drive.

All the debate and delay about hospital expansion in the seven years since I had become county judge had quickly been resolved. Once the hospital's board had acted, the Commissioners Court took only two months to complete its part.

We finally were under way on by far the most comprehensive and costly expansion of the hospital system in its long history. Doug McMurry, executive vice president for the San Antonio Chapter of Associated General Contractors, said that winning the construction contract would be like winning the Super Bowl.

In January 2009 the hospital board approved a design that was both functional and cost effective. Mark Webb, vice president for facilities development, said the ten-story glass and steel hospital would be trimmed in Pecos red limestone. The two older buildings would be refurbished.

The design of the Sky Tower at University Hospital would be LEED-certified to ensure lower energy and maintenance costs. Patient rooms would be larger, with more natural light. The Air-LIFE helipad would be on top of the hospital instead of the parking garage, enabling patients to be moved more quickly.

In May 2009 the hospital board awarded the contract for building the ten-story tower and remodeling two existing buildings. An additional floor was added during construction to provide for possible future expansion.

Some six months later, construction began on the 212,000-square-foot outpatient building downtown. The facilities would handle a 365 percent increase from the current 130,000 yearly patient visits. A remaining historic building on the site would be converted into a larger pharmacy to increase prescriptions by forty thousand annually.

On January 13, 2013, the downtown six-story clinical facility opened on the Robert B. Green campus. The grand brick building included a computerized LED light sculpture by Bill FitzGibbons around the top edge that lit up the city's night skyline. The inside, featuring striking sculptures and paintings throughout, included 162 examining rooms and 21 advanced treatment rooms. The clinic had the best of equipment, including two new MRI scans and six new CT scans. An extra floor provided room for future growth.

Fourteen months later, on a cold, windy day in March 2014, we held grand opening ceremonies for the Sky Tower in the medical center. Everyone gathered under the huge elongated portico in front of the building, which was like standing in a wind tunnel. The cold wind inspired us to keep our remarks short.

The tower's front was stunning: it featured sheets of glass in alternating colors—blue, white, and transparent—patterned to resemble the sky. On the opposite wall of the portico, local artist Riley Robinson had painted thousands of bluebonnets.

Several of us made short speeches, and Dr. William Henrich, president of the Health Science Center, summed it up best: "This hospital exceeds our wildest expectations in size, function, and beauty."

Then we walked into a large lobby surrounded by outstanding works of art. To the right was a netlike sculpture dotted with colorful disks representing foxglove, source of the lifesaving heart drug digitalis. To the left, a series of crimson plates showed the face of Hippocrates, the father of Western medicine. Above was an expanse of glass with strands of color representing DNA.

Throughout the hospital were more than one thousand original works of art and design enhancements, and for good reason. A 2009 report by the Society for Arts in Healthcare found that art is healing and results in shorter hospital stays, less medication, and fewer complications. Art also improves workplace satisfaction and reduces anxiety.

We then visited a few of the 420 new private rooms, which included an interactive entertainment/patient education system. Likewise, the thirty-five surgical suites included state-of-the-art technology, allowing doctors instantly to pull up X-rays and laboratory results or to refer to electronic medical records.

We also enjoyed the two rooftop gardens, which featured Texas wildflowers and native grasses. Watered with condensation from the air-conditioning system, these gardens helped cool off the building. Along with its green technology, the building was certified as LEED Gold, an environmental recognition rare among hospitals.

Doubling the size of the emergency center assured citizens of care without long waits, enabling the hospital to serve some 2 million people in the surrounding twenty-two counties.

Once we had completed the hospital and the downtown clinical ambulatory building, the University Health System was ready for the future. It had gleaming buildings, state-of-the-art equipment, and the capacity to more than double or triple business over the next few decades.

We also reserved land for a building that could be attached to the Sky Tower. But at that point it was unclear how that building would be built and what medical services would be performed in it. A rocky road, one with many twists and turns, still lay before us as we sought a partnership to build a children's hospital. It would eventually have a huge impact on the Sky Tower and the proposed attached building.

## A CHILDREN'S HOSPITAL

In 2008, the same year that the Commissioners Court approved financing for the hospital and clinical building, I jumped into another controversial proposal. I was invited by Nancy Ray, chief nurse executive at University Hospital, to speak at an annual ceremony honoring nurses. I spoke of the need to build a critical care children's hospital.

There were fifty such hospitals nationwide, and San Antonio was the only major American city without one. A first-class hospital that serves only children can offer specialized care for youngsters with complex and rare medical conditions. As a teaching hospital with an academic affiliation, it participates in research and clinical trials. A foundation associated with the hospital raises private funds to support research.

San Antonio was losing its best and brightest subspecialty pediatric doctors to other children's hospitals. Subspecialty doctors, in addition to providing critical care, also drive research.

After my speech, I asked Hernandez to commission a feasibility study on building a children's hospital. At his recommendation, his board supported funding the study.

In September 2009 officials from all the hospitals, as well as several doctors and community representatives, joined us at a press conference to release the conclusion of the study by Kurt Salmon Associates of San Bruno, California. The study found that San Antonio had a large and growing population of children that would support a children's hospital if at least two of the city's four largest hospitals would partner on the project.

Besides University Hospital, the major hospital systems are Christus Santa Rosa Health Care System, owned by Christus Health, located in Dallas; Methodist Healthcare, owned by HCA, based in Nashville; and Baptist Health System, then owned by Vanguard Health Systems of Nashville, based in Dallas.

Santa Rosa and Methodist Hospitals had made a previous attempt to build a children's hospital in the early 1990s. The partnership wanted to keep emergency services, neonatal, and outpatient services downtown at the existing Santa Rosa Hospital. Tertiary long-term care would take place in a new hospital in the medical center near the UT Health Science Center.

But the plan ran into trouble when sixty doctors associated with Santa Rosa opposed moving children's services to the medical center. The board of the University Health System opposed a children's hospital, fearing it would rob services from the county hospital district.

The situation worsened when US Representative Henry B. Gonzalez threatened to withhold federal funds until he received proof that the partnership was committed to downtown. Four months after Gonzalez's statement, the partnership broke up over internal differences, uncertainties about federal funding, and the battle over location.

Eighteen years after the Methodist–Santa Rosa partnership had failed, we again were proposing a partnership to build a children's hospital. Jim Adams, one of my three hospital district board appointees, took the lead in sorting out the complexities of a partnership with another hospital. Adams had been president of the International Division for AT&T and was chairman of Texas Instruments.

He thought Methodist would be the strongest financial partner. Since the 1990s, it had grown its pediatric services from a 3 percent market share to 40 percent. But Methodist did not express serious interest.

Trip Pilgrim, CEO of the regional Baptist Health System, said he was ready to form a partnership, but Baptist had the smallest market share, and the hospital district board did not give it serious consideration.

Dr. Tom Mayes, chief of pediatrics at Santa Rosa and chairman of the Department of Pediatrics at the UT Health Science Center, thought the hospital district should partner with Santa Rosa. As you may recall, the hospital district had lost its pediatric unit to Santa Rosa in 1999. Some one hundred pediatric doctors associated with the Health Science Center were practicing at Santa Rosa, which held a 24 percent market share of children services.

As Adams was sorting through the possible partnerships, we visited children's hospitals across the nation, meeting with their top officials. We visited three children's hospitals in New York City (Presbyterian, Montefiore, and Mount Sinai), and others in Omaha and Oklahoma City. We learned a great deal about how to best build and operate a children's hospital.

After analyzing the possible partnerships, Adams determined that the best opportunity lay with Santa Rosa. Unlike the other two local hospital systems, it was a nonprofit, as we were. Most children's hospitals were nonprofit. Thus we reached an agreement to move ahead with the partnership.

On December 17, 2010, we all signed a letter of intent at a public meeting at the Commissioners Court. I was elated and confident the community soon would have its first critical care children's hospital.

The partnership engaged Blue Cottage Consulting to help develop a business plan, strategic roadmap, governance model, and financial expectations, as well as size and location of the hospital.

Over the next several months, while the partnership tried to reach a final agreement, I met monthly with business community leaders to build support. Mayes, Hernandez, and Santa Rosa CEO Pat Carrier joined me at those meetings.

We explained the need for the hospital to be in the medical center. The UT Health Science Center was located there, of course, and most of the pediatricians practiced in the center or nearby. But the proposed partnership made slow progress. Christus Health in Dallas experienced leadership changes—Ernie Sadau became the CEO, Gene Woods the COO—and those transitions caused delays. As talks dragged on, I expressed my frustration publicly.

Then, in September, a consulting group called to tell us that Christus Health was considering moving its headquarters from Dallas to Houston or San Antonio. Mayor Julián Castro and I followed up with a joint letter offering financial support for the move.

On December 2, 2011, Castro and I met with Sadau and Jeff Puckett, vice president of Christus Health. We proposed a downtown building vacated by AT&T as a site for its offices. We laid out a package of incentives totaling $12,761,700. Sadau said he was pleased with the offer and was serious about a possible move to San Antonio. Castro and I followed up with a letter that laid out the incentives.

The deal seemed like a slam-dunk. Fifty members of the headquarters team already worked at Santa Rosa in San Antonio. The hospital district was its partner on a proposed children's hospital. The organization did not have a hospital in Dallas. Archbishop Gustavo García-Siller wrote a letter of support.

As time passed, its leaders made additional demands about the downtown location. They wanted a lower rent, so we got the owner to reduce it. They wanted a parking garage, so the city agreed to build one.

Our letter of intent to partner on the children's hospital expired on January 1, 2012. But we continued to work with Christus Health, hoping we could reach an agreement and get them to move to San Antonio.

Then, on January 12, just two weeks before the organization would make the location decision, its leaders said they did not like the downtown building because the floor plates were too small. They had known about the size of those floor plates for several months, but had made no mention of them.

They said they liked a building that Valero Energy Co. owned and did not use. They said Valero did not want to rent to them. Not wanting to give up, I called Valero CEO Bill Klesse and told him how important the project was to San Antonio. He agreed to lease the building and submitted a proposal to them.

Fifteen days later they announced they would stay in Dallas and move fifty people out of San Antonio. Without a doubt, they were using us to get a better deal in Dallas.

Meanwhile, in late January the Blue Cottage report commissioned by the Christus/University partnership was released. It found that the children's hospital should be built in the medical center, and listed several potential sites. The report also laid out business and strategic plans.

But we still could not reach a deal with Christus: there were disagreements over who should manage the hospital and who should own the building. Christus also was concerned about the open record requirements of a public entity and the cost of a comprehensive academic program.

Our hospital board gave up and withdrew on March 1, 2012. The failure of the proposed partnership was a crushing blow in the attempt to bring two hospital systems together to build a children's hospital. As in any partnership, both partners shared blame for the failure.

After the Christus/University Hospital partnership failed, power flowed to the UT Health Science Center. It had to decide whether to keep its pediatric program with Christus Santa Rosa Hospital or move its pediatric affiliation to another hospital.

Pilgrim had been brushed aside when the Baptist system expressed interest a year earlier. He now entered center stage. On March 22, 2012, just twenty-one days after the county hospital board broke off talks with Christus, I met with Pilgrim at the Hotel Contessa.

"I am going to share some confidential information with you," he said, "but you must keep it secret." After I had agreed, he continued: "We are developing a nationwide partnership with the Children's Hospital of Philadelphia. They share with Boston Children's Hospital the number one ranking by *U.S. News and World Report*. We would be interested in University Hospital building the children's hospital, owning it and leasing it to our partnership."

"I assume you would affiliate with the UT Health Science Center," I said. When he answered yes, I noted, "That would put you in a confrontation with Santa Rosa." He nodded.

"This could be very interesting," I said. "The Children's Hospital of Philadelphia would bring immediate credibility."

On April 12 Pilgrim met with Henrich, Adams, and Hernandez. Adams expressed frustration about not being included earlier in the talks. He advised Henrich not to sign an affiliation agreement until the proposed partnership had been firmed up and funding for the hospital construction had been identified.

Adams still did not want to give up on Methodist. So a few days later we met with Kevin Moriarty, CEO of Methodist Healthcare Ministries, and Dudley Harral, its former board president. Moriarty said, "We are working on a plan whereby private pediatric physicians would conjunctionally staff the children's hospital with University of Texas medical school doctors."

"That won't be easy," I said. Approximately 450 private pediatric physicians practiced at Methodist. Some 150 pediatric physicians are associated with the UT Medical School. There has always been distrust between the two groups.

Moriarty said, "Our foundation will encourage them. We will pledge a $100 million gift to the new children's hospital to be paid out over a ten-year period. We need another five months to complete a physician integration plan and to get approval from HCA."

Adams said, "Time will run out if you don't move faster."

"We will try," Harral replied.

A few days later, Pilgrim wrote a letter to Hernandez and Henrich saying that Vanguard and the Children's Hospital of Philadelphia, or CHOP, would provide a proposal within sixty days to build the children's hospital and comprehensive pediatric care network. The story made the front page of the *San Antonio Express-News*.

The next day, Christus announced it was planning to close its downtown adult hospital and commit $135 million to convert the sixty-year-old building into a freestanding children's hospital. It expected the Health Science Center to keep its affiliation with them.

In mid-July Methodist officials met with the Health Science Center team. They said they would build a 150-bed tower attached to their current children's hospital. They said a plan to integrate the medical school's pediatrics department still had not been determined.

For the next month, everyone continued to refine their plans as the Health Science Center team evaluated them. Dr. Kenneth Kalkwarf became interim president because Henrich was undergoing a health challenge. Michael Black, COO, and Dr. Francisco González-Scarano, medical school dean, rounded out the leadership team.

On July 28, I met with Kalkwarf, Black, and González-Scarano at Jim's Restaurant on Loop 410 and Blanco. They told me they all supported the alliance with Vanguard and CHOP. González-Scarano had worked for CHOP at one time and knew many of its officials.

A few weeks later Gene Powell, chairman of the UT Board of Regents, called to invite me to a meeting of the board at the South Texas Research Facility on September 7. Of course, I knew where the UT ship was headed.

Vanguard-Baptist, HCA-Methodist, and University Hospital officials were represented at the meeting. Christus Santa Rosa officials knew what was coming and chose not to attend. One by one, Powell's fellow regents were conferenced in by phone.

Kalkwarf presented to the board a matrix of the three Methodist, Vanguard/CHOP, and Santa Rosa proposals. He recommended Vanguard/CHOP. Then Dr. Kenneth Shine, executive vice chancellor for health affairs, cited a Vanguard commitment of $75 million to establish a network of pediatric clinics throughout South Texas. He said the partnership had committed $350 million for a freestanding, licensed, academic-based, 205-bed children's hospital at the medical center. He also cited a commitment for financial support for education and research.

The unanimous vote that quickly followed directed Dr. Francisco Cigarroa, who by then was chancellor of the UT System, and his team to complete the affiliation agreement with Vanguard/CHOP.

After the meeting, in a quickly gathered press conference, I said I supported the board's decision. I said that the hospital district would continue to talk with Vanguard/CHOP about any possible relationship.

Afterward Pilgrim told me, "The affiliation agreement has to be completed, land acquired, plans drawn up, and then we have to build and open it. You could say the vote today was a leap of faith."

Later Santa Rosa announced that it would enter into an affiliation agreement with Baylor College of Medicine and a partnership with Texas Children's Hospital in Houston. It said Health Science Center doctors should vacate Santa Rosa by the following July. It also threatened to sue. Things were getting nasty.

As 2013 circled around, the Vanguard/CHOP proposal crawled forward slower than a turtle. Doctors at the medical school were nervous because they were required to vacate the Santa Rosa facility by the end of June, and as yet had no place to move their practices. The Health Science Center had made no contingency plans with Vanguard for the fallout from their termination of their affiliation with Christus.

When the medical school turned to the hospital district for temporary help, the hospital board did not jump at the opportunity. The board had been excluded from the Vanguard/CHOP discussions from the very beginning and thought this was not its problem.

In the end, hospital board members decided it was in the district's best interest to assist them, for several reasons. First, the Health Science Center's presence in the community is unrivaled in importance. It is primarily responsible for the city's booming health care industry, a prime economic generator. Second, it is the hospital district's partner and thus necessary to the success of University Hospital. Finally, the board understood that inner-city pediatric physicians were scarce and that the opportunity to help the medical school graduate more pediatricians was in the community's best interest. Even though the Health Science Center treats the district badly from time to time, the hospital district stands by it.

And there was another reason for them to give the temporary help. Remember the land we reserved next to the Sky Tower for an attached building? With the UT Health Science Center being forced out of Santa Rosa Hospital and the uncertainty concerning the Vanguard/CHOP proposal, the idea of such a building now came into sharper focus as a possibility for a children's hospital. It would be described as "free-leaning," meaning that it would be separate but connected to critical services located in the Sky Tower.

Soon the Health Science Center would need the hospital district more than ever: a big bomb was about to be dropped on the proposed Vanguard/CHOP partnership. On June 24, 2013, Tenet Healthcare announced it was buying Vanguard for $1.8 billion in cash. Dallas-based Tenet had twenty-eight hospitals, and when the sale closed, it would have seventy-nine.

Tenet CEO Trevor Fetter assured me the organization would move forward with the plan to build a children's hospital. But there was one little problem he didn't mention: Tenet competed with the Children's Hospital of Philadelphia. CHOP soon notified Tenet it was exercising its right to exit the partnership.

Vanguard leaders had to have known at least several months before the Tenet announcement that they would sell their hospital to the company that competed with CHOP. Yet they led all of us to believe that things were going fine.

Adams was right when he warned UT Health Science Center officials not to sign an affiliation agreement with Baptist/CHOP until all commitments were in place.

Not wanting to give up, UT officials continued to talk to Tenet and Methodist for months, to no avail.

In the end, they finally grabbed the county hospital district's hand and said they wanted to affiliate their pediatric program with it. More than 110 pediatric doctors and 40 resident/fellows affiliated with the Health Science Center returned to University Hospital. They joined a few resident and faculty doctors who had stayed to handle trauma, burns, and premature babies.

Dr. Mayes had told me several times that when the partnership with Vanguard/CHOP blew up, UT doctors wanted to return to University Hospital. The UT Board of Regents and the local administration dragged their feet, which were probably made of clay.

Santa Rosa closed its downtown adult hospital and remodeled the building into a freestanding children's hospital called the Children's Hospital of San Antonio. Its new affiliation with Baylor College of Medicine has brought new medical talent to San Antonio.

Although our original joint study showed that the children's hospital should have been in the medical center, Santa Rosa pushed ahead with the downtown development. Ironically, our six-story clinical building, staffed by University of Texas pediatricians, provided outpatient services for children only a few blocks away. Those children who needed to be transferred to a hospital would naturally go our new hospital at the medical center.

As the remodeling of Santa Rosa Hospital got under way, I became acquainted with its new leadership and met several doctors affiliated with Baylor College of Medicine. They are good doctors, and I hope Santa Rosa will be successful with their freestanding children's hospital. When I spoke at the opening ceremony of the Children's Hospital of San Antonio in June 2016,

I related some of the events that led to the creation of Santa Rosa's children's hospital.

The UT Health Science Center now has an academic rival at Santa Rosa. To be competitive, our hospital district stepped up to provide facilities and equipment for its pediatric practice within the Sky Tower. We committed seventy-two beds on the seventh floor, which had originally been planned for adult beds.

The hospital district developed a separate pediatric emergency department, new pediatric operating rooms, a designated unit for pediatric heart patients, and a center for pediatric patients with cancer and blood disorders. One of my three appointments to the board—Dr. Dianna M. Burns-Banks, a pediatrician—provided leadership in establishing the program.

The hospital district also agreed to invest the necessary funds for a highly trained medical team and technology to be recognized as a Level 1 Pediatric Trauma Center by the American College of Surgeons. The number of seriously injured children treated at University Hospital has risen 78 percent in the last five years. In June 2016 the American College of Surgeons recognized the facility as the first and only Level 1 Pediatric Trauma Center in South Texas. This puts it in the elite company of Level 1 centers in Houston, Dallas, and Austin.

With pediatric services now solidified with University Hospital, Hernandez pushed ahead with a plan to build a six-story women's and children's tower connected to the Sky Tower. It would include 250 new and replacement beds for neonatal intensive care, pediatrics, obstetrics, gynecology, and shell space for future growth. The pediatric operating rooms would remain in the Sky Tower as well as the designated unit for pediatric heart patients.

Having women and children services in a separate building would give those services their own identity and enable better and more efficient care. At the same time, all support services in the Sky Tower would be available via a hallway.

In July 2017 the Board of Managers unanimously approved the plans for building. This would be the only women and children's hospital in San Antonio.

The plans also included finishing out forty-three thousand square feet in the Sky Tower that had been shelled out for future use. A Heart and Vascular Institute would be located in the vacant space, with cardiac cath labs, diagnostic cardiology, and interventional radiology. It would also provide space for advanced endoscopy procedures. More than sixty-five liver transplants were performed at the hospital in 2016.

The total cost of the project was $390 million, including $330 million for the women's and children's tower, $40 million for the Heart and Vascular Institute and Advanced Endoscopy, and $20 million for a parking garage expansion. It would be paid for with $82 million from the hospital's reserve and $308 million in bonds. The financing would not include a tax increase.

On July 26 Commissioner Paul Elizondo and I teamed up with Hernandez and his team—VP/COO Ed Banos, VP/CFO Reed Hurley, VP/Strategic Communications Leni Kirkman, interim medical school dean Dr. Ronald Rodriguez, and Chief of Staff Kristen Plastino—to present our case to the *Express-News* editorial board, headed by O. Ricardo Pimentel.

Dr. Plastino, who is also a professor of OB/GYN, made a compelling argument about why the women's and children's hospital was necessary. Dr. Rodriguez said that the state-of-the-art Sky Tower had enabled him to attract top medical talent from around the country and that the Women's and Children's Hospital would bring many talented pediatric subspecialists to our city. Hurley assured the board that we had the capacity to amortize the debt, and Banos said our operational efficiency would improve.

I stated that the Commissioners Court planned to vote on the financing plan on August 8. I added that I had complete confidence in Hernandez and his team in view of the fact that they had proved that the building and operation of the Sky Tower was successful. Commissioner Elizondo said that we needed to serve the poor with top-quality women's and children's services.

On August 8 the Commissioners Court met and took the first step toward approval by giving a thirty-day public notice of intent to issue the certificates or obligation. The vote was unanimous in favor of moving forward.

## CHALLENGES FOR THE FUTURE

The Institute of Medicine found that those who are uninsured receive about half the medical care of those covered by insurance. Because they don't have coverage, the uninsured wait until they are very sick before they seek help at our hospital. These more serious medical conditions require more expensive treatment.

Texas is the second-worst state in the nation for insurance coverage; nearly one-third of our citizens lack coverage. Reimbursements rates for Medicaid and Medicare are near the bottom. The state's horrible record places a great burden on local hospital districts to serve the working poor.

In 2009 help seemed to be on the way when Congress began debate on the Affordable Care Act (ACA). It provided expansion for Medicaid and people who exceeded the income provision for Medicaid would be able to buy subsidized insurance.

At a dinner in Washington, DC, right after the House passed the bill on October 8, I thanked our congressional delegation for its support, saying that if Medicaid was expanded, we would finally see a significant improvement in health care in Texas and would be able to cut hospital taxes. In December the Senate passed the bill with some amendments, which the House approved on March 21, 2010. Two days later President Barack Obama signed the ACA into law. This was the most important health legislation since the passage of Medicare and Medicaid in 1965.

But Republicans hated the ACA and began an intensive campaign to denigrate the legislation, dubbing it Obamacare. Many states governed by Republicans filed lawsuits to prevent implementation of the act. On June 28, 2012, the US Supreme Court upheld the ACA's constitutionality but ruled that individual states could choose not to expand Medicaid coverage.

Most of us thought that no state would turn down Medicaid expansion—especially not Texas, where more than 30 percent of the citizens had no health insurance coverage. But we were wrong. In this strong red state where Republicans controlled both houses as well as all statewide elected offices, politics conquered common sense. Texas refused to participate; instead, it let federal funds flow to other states.

We did our best to change the minds of legislators and the governor. I joined my fellow county judges, who were responsible for their respective hospital districts, in urging the legislature to expand Medicaid. We also held press conferences with COPS/Metro Alliance to push for passage. I emphasized that Bexar County Hospital District would collect some $54 million annually, enabling us to cut hospital taxes by about 15 percent. Texas was passing up $6 billion annually from the federal government.

We never made it to first base. Not a single Republican in a leadership position spoke up for Medicaid expansion. So we pressed ahead with enrolling citizens for the insurance available under the ACA. Texas refused to set up a state exchange program whereby citizens could shop for insurance coverage, so we had to rely on the federal exchange program.

Mayor Julián Castro and I held a press conference on February 5, 2014, to launch the enrollment campaign. Despite lack of state support and federal website problems, some seventy-six thousand people in Bexar County enrolled during the first enrollment phase.

In November Sylvia Burwell, newly appointed Health and Human Services secretary, visited San Antonio to allay citizens' concerns about another Republican lawsuit. This time the Republicans sought to prevent citizens in states that had not created exchanges from having the right to receive tax credits on their insurance. Because Texas had not set up a state exchange, all the citizens we had signed up could lose their tax credits.

At the New Creation Church in Windcrest, Burwell said she was confident that the Supreme Court would uphold the right to receive tax credits, and her prediction proved to be right. Seven months later, on June 25, 2015, the US Supreme Court, in a 6–3 vote, upheld the right to tax credits even if a state refused to enact an exchange. It was a day of jubilation.

In fall 2014 we kicked off the second enrollment phase at a Main Plaza rally. By the end of the second enrollment period, the ACA proved to be a great success in Texas despite lack of state support. More than 6 million Texans enrolled.

But this was only a partial victory. Texas still refuses to expand Medicaid. I hope that one day the Republican leadership in Texas will come to its senses and expand coverage under Medicaid.

After insurance coverage under the ACA, only 16 percent of Bexar County citizens did not have insurance coverage in 2015, down from 23 percent uninsured in 2014. During the same time frame, participation in the hospital district's CareLink declined from 40,685 patients in 2014 to 26,994 in 2015. As a result, University Hospital's cost of uncompensated care dropped 23 percent from $102 million in 2014 to $78 million in 2015.

While the ACA has been helpful, Medicaid expansion would enable many more people to be covered. But it is unlikely that Texas will expand Medicaid, certainly not after the election of Donald Trump. He campaigned against ACA insurance coverage, and now Congress, after trying and failing to repeal and replace the ACA, is attempting to kill it by repealing the requirement that individuals must either buy insurance or pay a fine.

In addition to the uncertainty regarding ACA there is concern regarding federal supplemental payment programs like disproportionate share (DSH), the Network Access Improvement Program (NAIP), and the 1115 Waiver.

Bexar County as of fiscal year 2017 provides more than $400 million in yearly funding to the hospital district through the hospital tax that the Commissioners Court assesses and is responsible for. Teaching hospitals also do not have to pay property taxes like other hospitals. So while we have to take care of anyone walking in the door, our hospital district has the advantage of strong support from the Commissioners Court.

Even with the support of Bexar County hospital taxes, the hospital district has to remain focused on getting paying clients. They have a higher percentage of paying clients than any other hospital district in Texas. They also have to stay focused on increasing business through expanding services. In the last negotiation with the UT Health Science Center, we reserved the right to open up the hospital to private physicians, because private physicians can bring the hospital many paying patients.

To stay competitive and offer the best of services, University Health System must also stay on top of rapidly changing medical technologies. And they are doing that. Their Neonatal Nutrition and Bone Institute, which specializes in providing optimal care for premature infants, is the nation's first such facility. Real-time online video and communication technology allow parents to see their babies in the neonatal intensive care unit at any time.

The emergency department is equipped with technology unmatched in the region. It has a 128-slice CT scanner, laboratory, and X-ray for fast and accurate diagnosis of injuries. It has high-resolution video displays and touch-screen controls so that surgical teams can examine X-rays on a large wall-mounted monitor. It also has videoconferencing.

Patients can watch videos on the television in their room to learn about their health problems. A state-of-the-art call system allows patients to reach their nurses wherever they are in the hospital. Bill Phillips, chief information officer, developed plans for a Tier III Data Center, which was completed and turned into the primary data center for the health system.

For the past seven years, University Health System has been named one of the nation's most wired hospitals by *Hospitals and Health Networks* magazine. The comprehensive electronic health records system means every provider at every University Health System location has immediate access.

We must continue to expand the hospital system's fifteen neighborhood outpatient centers, which educate our clients on the need for checkups, a proper diet, and exercise and also serve as a pipeline for our hospital for seriously ill patients. In November 2016, we held a groundbreaking ceremony for an outpatient clinic on the East Side. Commissioner Tommy Calvert, who was elected in 2014, became the first African American to serve on the court. A graduate of Tufts University, he became a major proponent of the clinic. Hospital board members Smith and Burns-Banks were also key supporters.

The hospital system also operates three Express-Med urgent care centers, two outpatient surgery centers, four outpatient renal dialysis centers, and a world-class center for diabetes research and education.

It must continue to enhance patient services including preventive health care measures. An example of our health education programs is the media and education campaign that warns people on the hazards of consuming too much sugar. I persuaded the Commissioners Court to launch the campaign under the leadership Bryan Alsip, University Health System's chief medical officer, and Leni Kirkman, senior vice president of strategic communication and patient relations. We partnered with the Bexar County Health Collaborative in a multimedia campaign highlighting the amount of sugar in colas and other soft drinks. We will continue to look for ways to educate people on preventive health care.

As this book goes to press, the University Health System is well positioned for the future. The hospital system has more than seven thousand employees, with an annual budget of $1.5 billion. It has more than eight hundred physicians and resident physicians working side by side to provide around-the-clock care. As an academic hospital, it has the most specialized and advanced services for complex illnesses and injuries in all major specialties. It is on the leading edge in training doctors and health care professionals for the future. Seven hundred resident physicians in fifty-one accredited medical training programs rotate through the hospital. More than 1,800 medical, allied health, and nursing students use these facilities. The hospital also conducts research and develops technology.

University Hospital has won numerous awards and recognition nationwide. *U.S. News and World Report* ranks it as the best hospital in San Antonio and the sixth best hospital in Texas. In 2016 it ranked among the top fifty in kidney and gynecology and was also recognized for high performance in cancer, colon cancer, heart failure, chronic obstructive pulmonary disease, and urology.

The American Nurses Credentialing Center has recognized University Health System with magnet status, its gold standard for quality of patient care; University is the first and only health care organization in South Texas with that recognition. The University Transplant Center has twice received a Medal of Honor from the US Department of Health and Human and Services for patient outcomes exceeding the national average for kidney, liver, and lung transplantation.

As things stand now, the pathway toward the future is bright as the county hospital system strives to bring the best health care services to anyone who walks through the health system's doors.

# FOUR

## *Therapeutic Justice*

WHEN I BECAME MAYOR in 1991, violent crime was rampant in San Antonio, as in many other American cities. Since 1978 drugs and gang turf wars, both youth and adult, had caused crime to increase steadily and significantly.

In 1990 the city had experienced 219 homicides, a record number. In May 1991, when I took office, the rate was exceeding the previous year's.

That December Mayor Steve Bartlett of Dallas, Mayor Bruce Todd of Austin, and I teamed up to form Mayors United on Safety, Crime, and Law Enforcement (MUSCLE), expanding the organization to include mayors of the eight largest Texas cities. The cities contributed funds to staff and operate MUSCLE, which was tasked with creating a plan to fight crime and lobbying the Texas legislature to pass measures to implement the plan.

During meetings in 1992, with input from law enforcement agencies, we developed a twelve-point program to control crime. The top goals were building additional prison cells and developing a priority system to keep violent offenders in prison longer.

Plan in hand, I drove to Austin for the opening day of the

1993 Texas legislature. As I drove up Congress Avenue toward the impressive 311-foot-high red granite and limestone Texas Capitol, I recalled fond memories from my days in the legislature. On my way to the House of Representatives chamber, I passed my old House and Senate offices. Because I am a former member of both houses, I have floor privileges that allow me to approach legislators in the chambers. Thus I could meet with many of them in a relatively short time. Both as mayor and later as a county judge, I took advantage of this privilege.

After visiting with some of the 150 House members about the legislative agenda to fight crime, I headed for the smaller and more elegant Senate, with its thirty-one desks. Again, I worked the floor.

After several lobbying trips, the coalition of mayors succeeded in pushing the legislature to submit to voters a bond package to build thirty-four thousand prison beds. The coalition supported the initiative, and voters overwhelmingly passed it. This was the first stage of a large Texas prison expansion during the late 1990s.

The coalition also secured passage of a bill that required every convicted felon sentenced to a life term must serve thirty years before eligibility for parole. "Good time" points could not reduce the thirty years. Another bill clarified that judges had the right to set higher bails if the accused was a threat to the public. During two legislative sessions, most of the coalition's anticrime bills passed.

Meanwhile, back home I stepped up the local fight against crime. With support from the city council, I set up a twenty-nine-member Crime Prevention Commission.

Based on its recommendations, the city developed an anti-graffiti ordinance and a Cellular on Patrol program providing civilians with cell phones programmed with a direct line to the police. We also started a Citizen Police Academy to teach people how to implement prevention programs. We opened police substations and created a working relationship between the police and neighborhood leaders.

Voters approved spending $17 million to build a police technology center that included a state-of-the-art fingerprint identification system and communication equipment. Representatives of the gang unit, bomb squad, and SWAT team special operations were stationed in the facility. The police department created downtown foot and bike patrols, a domestic violence unit, and foot patrols in housing projects.

In early 1993 I talked with Police Chief Bill Gibson about concentrating forces in the worst crime areas during peak crime hours. He created a 102-member violent crime task force, backed by a 141-member investigative task force.

Apprehensions for violent crimes soared in the last six months of the year to 840 felony arrests, with the seizure of 295 weapons and five thousand rounds of ammunition. Thanks to the crackdown, overall crime decreased in 1993.

Along with getting tough on crime, we also created prevention programs aimed at youth. We created a Youth Commission of twenty-two students in grades 10 through 12, which made several recommendations regarding youth recreation programs. We launched "Operation Cool It" at thirty-five sites for Night Owl recreation programs and extended swimming pool hours. The council increased the budget for youth programs by $10 million to $50 million.

We started the Coalition, a public/private organization made up of the city, agencies serving youth, local media, the business community, and the Youth Commission. We created logos such as "Improve your hang time," "Kick it," and "Join the Co." More than thirty thousand young people signed up the first summer. We also began an after-school-care program, starting with twenty schools and expanding to sixty before I left office. Kids could stay at school until 5:30 p.m., allowing parents to pick them up after work.

We received a $1.5 million federal grant through the Justice Department's Weed and Seed initiative to use for youth programs. Attorney General Janet Reno and I toured the East Side to see them in action. I believe these youth programs were significant in lowering juvenile crime to the rates we see today. We won three national awards for youth programs.

With the support of the Youth Commission, we passed a midnight curfew for juveniles. The ordinance established parental fines. Parents and youth quickly got the word: during the ordinance's first six months, 481 youths were arrested. So young people stayed at home. During the first two years, juvenile crime victimization went down 53 percent, and during curfew hours, juvenile crime decreased 77 percent.

I was very pleased that during my two mayoral terms the city made major strides in addressing crime by apprehending and punishing violent offenders and establishing prevention programs.

By the time I became county judge six years later in May 2001, Texas had spent $2.3 billion to triple the state prison system's capacity to more than 150,000 beds. The Texas prison population, along with the inmates in 273 county jails, had increased approximately sixfold since 1978, the year crime began to rise. Texas had become one of five states with the highest rates of incarcerated people.

Although crime had declined each year in the last ten years, the state still had an overcrowded prison and jail system. Bexar County's jail was crammed with around 4,500 inmates. A study given to me when I took office recommended that the jail capacity be expanded to make room for even more inmates. I wanted to get a better understanding of the jail population before deciding what to do. Incarcerating people is very expensive, which is one reason why only those who present a threat to the public should be locked up and why, as mayor, I had focused on incarcerating violent criminals. With some nine hundred detention officers, the jail's annual budget was approximately $50 million.

Touring the jail, I noted the large population of nonviolent drug dependent and mentally ill inmates. University Hospital psychiatrists were doing their best to treat the many ill inmates in harsh jail conditions. But prisoners had the right to refuse medication, and many chose to do so. I heard inmates screaming behind locked doors. The psychiatrist on duty told me that 35 to 40 percent of the inmates had either a drug addiction or mental illness or both. The county's University Hospital was spending approximately $9 million annually to treat detainees in the jail and juvenile detention center. Doctors made more than ninety thousand visits each year either to jail clinics or to the hospital's secure ward. I quickly grasped that nonviolent drug addicts and the mentally ill should be diverted from jail and treated in hospitals and clinics rather than in jail or prison.

The problem of incarcerating mentally ill people dated back to the 1960s, when thousands of patients were released from state psychiatric hospitals. During the 1950s some four thousand patients were in the San Antonio State Hospital. Today it holds fewer than three hundred.

The development of antipsychotic drugs had offered a false hope that these people could be treated as outpatients. But instead many mentally ill people go untreated, living on the streets or ending up in jail. Those with severe symptoms are taken to hospital emergency rooms, usually to the county's University Hospital, which averages 180 such patients a month. The hospital has twenty beds for those needing inpatient stabilization.

As mayor, I had learned about dealing with violent crime and punishment. I also had grasped the importance of prevention programs. But as county judge, I faced a very different problem. I needed to understand the third major component of fighting crime: treatment and rehabilitation.

After learning as much as possible, I told my colleagues on the Commissioners Court that I would not support adding jail capacity. I encouraged fellow commissioners to explore how we could change the system to help nonviolent offenders rather than incarcerate them. I found a great ally in Commissioner Paul Elizondo, who had a long history of advocating for mental health treatment.

Even though crime problems had changed from violent to nonviolent, the Republican-dominated legislature was not willing to recognize the difference. Members would have to be convinced that too many nonviolent people who were sick with drug addiction and mental illness should be treated rather than imprisoned. I would need the support of local judges who were interested in therapeutic justice and willing to focus on treatment rather than incarceration. I also needed support from the various health care agencies.

Two of the largest local health care agencies were associated with Bexar County: the Bexar County Hospital District (dba University Hospital) and the Bexar County Center for Health

Care Services. The Commissioners Court appoints the board members for both organizations, provides part of their funding, and approves their budgets.

When I was a member of the Texas legislature, I had worked with the Center for Health Care Services when I had passed a law that established the methadone maintenance program, which provided a pathway for people to get off heroin that is still used today. The center also ran several other programs to help people with mental health and substance abuse problems. With thirty-one clinics and facilities and nine hundred employees, it was critical to setting up treatment through a therapeutic justice program.

Before becoming county judge, I had chaired a task force to explore how to integrate the services of the hospital district and center. We recommended a plan for overlapping board members and sharing the hospital district's revenue with the Center for Health Care Services.

Leon Evans, director of the center, was ready to lead an effort to treat people rather than incarcerate them. He told me about the success of drug courts, first implemented in Dade County, Florida, in 1989. My friend Al Alonso, a county court-at-law judge, also had studied drug courts at the National Judicial College at the University of Nevada. He had become convinced that Bexar County should initiate a drug court. He suggested that the county create a misdemeanor adult drug court that would utilize judicial power to help rehabilitate drug addicts. Instead of sending defendants to jail, the judge could assign them to a rehabilitation program for up to eighteen months. Defendants would receive drug treatment counseling and attend weekly meetings. The judge would require participants to take drug tests and report to him as often as twice a week. Those who did not respond to rehabilitation would be sent to jail.

This would require that prosecutors, the defense bar, probation, law enforcement, mental health agencies, and social service agencies work together to help defendants cure their addiction and become productive citizens. Alonso found some skeptics. Some defense attorneys and assistant district attorneys did not want to be involved in rehabilitation. But the Commissioners Court supported him and authorized a budget to get the court up and running. The Center for Health Care Services provided much of the needed support.

Two years later, in 2003, Alonso reported to the Commissioners Court that he had more than 150 drug addicts in the program. For those who had completed it, the recidivism rate was less than 10 percent, a better success rate than most drug treatment programs throughout the nation. This not only reduced the jail population but also stabilized families and helped prevent people from being repeatedly arrested. The drug court also saved taxpayers a great deal of money. An inmate in the county jail cost taxpayers about $18,000 a year; a participant in the drug treatment program, $3,000.

In 2003 we also took steps to implement a jail diversion program. The Center for Health Care Services opened a twenty-four-hour crisis care facility on Leona Street near the hospital district's downtown Robert B. Green campus. Medical, psychiatric, and social work professionals staffed the facility.

The center worked with the police department and sheriff's office to establish an intensive training program for officers. During forty hours of training, officers learned how to identify and stabilize individuals with apparent mental health issues and safely de-escalate situations involving them. Officers who arrested nonviolent people with mental health problems took them to the center instead of to jail. There they were stabilized within twenty-four hours or, if needed, moved to longer treatment.

In addition to decreasing the jail population, diversion to treatment also provided relief both for emergency services at the hospital and police officers who often had to wait for hours in the emergency room with people they had arrested.

By 2005 the Center for Health Care Services had successfully diverted 4,100 mentally ill people from the jail into treatment programs. Within five years 17,000 had been diverted, saving some $50 million, and the program received a national award.

Based on the success of the misdemeanor drug court, district judges were ready in 2004 to create a felony drug court. Judge Mary Roman took on the difficult task of dealing with drug users accused of more serious offenses. Three years later, Ernie Glenn was hired as an associate judge to run the felony drug court. A former prosecutor and defense attorney, he had helped set up the felony drug court in 2004.

Within eight years, the felony drug court had evolved into a significant operation. Glenn presided over four dockets: the felony drug court; the felony reentry court; the felony co-occurring disorders court, for those with mental illness; and the felony DWI court. He screened clients and assigned them to the appropriate docket. Glenn's court has grown from a class of thirty in the graduating class of 2006 to seventy graduating each year. Over the last three years, for those who completed the program, the recidivism rate is only 13 percent—an incredible achievement.

Finally, in November 2006, state leaders began to pay attention to what the county was doing. Democratic senator John Whitmire and Republican Representative Jerry Madden, chairmen of the criminal justice committees in the Senate and the House, said that more than 154,000 people, the most in history, were in state prisons and jails. Although 59 percent of state prisoners were chemically dependent, only 5 percent received treatment. They said it was time for the state to look at rehabilitation, treatment, and parole for nonviolent offenders.

This was a major step: the state now recognized that punishment alone would not solve nonviolent criminal behavior. Legislators finally concluded they were contributing to more serious crime by incarcerating nonviolent mentally ill people with violent criminals who would have an adverse effect on their behavior. With a change in the state's policy, additional funding for treatment became available.

In 2008 the state stepped up to help the county, contributing some of the funding to open a detoxification center at 601 North Frio, across the street from the crisis care center for the mentally ill. The detoxification center had a twenty-bed sobering room and a fifteen-bed inpatient detox/counseling area. Police dropped off minor nonviolent offenders who needed to be dried out. The crisis center and the detoxification center later were consolidated and renamed the restoration center.

Also in 2008, Hardberger and I reached an agreement whereby the Bexar County Hospital District took over nine city public health clinics, absorbing 125 city employees. The nine clinics gave the county a greater capacity to care for the mentally ill and those addicted to drugs.

With the success of the drug courts, we began a series of other specialty courts to deal with mental health and alcohol abuse. In 2009 we created a misdemeanor mental health court, with individualized treatment programs, incentives for progress, and sanctions for noncompliance. The following year, we started the misdemeanor veteran's treatment court to work with veterans struggling with mental health disorders such as posttraumatic stress disorder.

Three years later we created a misdemeanor DWI court. Judge Liza Rodriguez began working with subsequent DWI offenders who were alcoholics, putting them into a treatment program. That same year we created a felony Esperanza Court to deal with people arrested for prostitution who had a drug or sex addiction or a mental health condition.

The Bexar County Community Supervision and Corrections Department supervises nineteen thousand offenders who have been put on probation, many of them from the specialty courts. Director Jarvis Anderson has reorganized the department to work with community organizations to provide a wide array of services including education programs and substance abuse and mental health services.

The department has created satellite offices to better serve those on probation. They also operate a three-hundred-bed substance abuse and mental health treatment facility on Applewhite Road. I have taken a tour of the facilities with Jarvis and met with numerous inmates. They are responding to treatment and those who finish the 120- to 180-day treatment have a success rate of 83 percent. By providing effective services the probation revocation rate has continued to go down even as the judges are putting more offenders on probation rather than incarcerating them.

In April 2010 we got some needed help from the city when it opened Haven for Hope, a thirty-seven-acre campus for the homeless on the near West Side. This was important because some 75 percent of people who live on the streets have mental health and drug problems. Many of them eventually end up in jail.

Haven for Hope includes a Prospects Courtyard that offers a safe place for the homeless to shower, eat, and sleep. The Center for Health Care Services runs the courtyard, offering medical care, therapy, and detoxification. Board member Mary Rose Brown, senior vice president at NuStar Energy, took the lead in organizing these services. If a homeless person wants to progress, he or she is offered follow-up medical treatment, including for mental illness and drug abuse, as well as an array of other services such as job training, counseling, and education.

Hardberger and Bill Greehey, CEO of NuStar Energy, were instrumental in funding and building community support for Haven for Hope. Through the years, the Commissioners Court has invested more than $14 million in the facility. We also have provided funding for people who have been arrested but need treatment rather than jail. This service has helped many people avoid the criminal justice system.

By creating six drug courts, a mental health court, a Veterans Court, a DWI court, an Esperanza Court, and jail diversion programs, the Commissioners Court has changed the Bexar County criminal justice system significantly to one that seeks to treat sick individuals rather than simply to incarcerate them.

This community is better off returning nonviolent people to society as productive members rather than breaking up families by jailing family members who suffer from drug addiction, mental health conditions, or both. In addition, dangerous inmates receive treatment in jail and assistance through a reentry program after they have served their terms, as I will explain later.

Unlike adult criminal justice, which focuses primarily on punishment, the juvenile system seeks to rehabilitate errant juveniles between the ages of ten and seventeen. A large Bexar County complex of buildings on Mitchell Street on San Antonio's South Side houses juvenile courts, a detention center, and new office buildings for juvenile probation that the Commissioners Court funded from a 2003 bond election. Three elected district judges and three associate judges have offices there.

Judge Laura Parker, who assumed office in 1999, was the administrative judge presiding over general jurisdiction courts as well as special dockets through 2016. She was instrumental in creating Crossroads Girls Mental Health Court, which addresses the mental health needs of girls ages twelve to seventeen. Created in 2009, her court received the 2016 National Criminal Justice Association's Outstanding Criminal Justice Program Award for the Western Region.

Parker ran the deferred prosecution drug court for first-time misdemeanor substance abuse. Her post-adjudication drug court has been a huge success. From 2006 to 2015, only 2 percent of the 250 juveniles who exited the program had subsequent abuse offenses.

Parker also chaired the Juvenile Board that oversees the juvenile probation department, the juvenile detention center, and the Cyndi Taylor Krier Juvenile Correctional Treatment Center. We named the complex after former county judge Cyndi Taylor Krier, who was instrumental in supporting programs to rehabilitate juveniles.

The juvenile probation department also operates an intake

office to decide whether to release young people who are arrested or to detain them in the detention center, which can house up to 278 juveniles. At the center, the San Antonio Independent School District offers classes, and the Bexar County Hospital District provides medical services. The judges then decide whether a young person should be sent to the juvenile correctional treatment center, a long-term treatment center with ninety-six beds that provides an array of educational and health services.

If the juvenile is released on probation, Lynne Wilkerson, juvenile probation director, sets up a program to help the young person. She oversees a staff trained in Motivational Interviewing skills, trauma care, and services that include aggression replacement training, family therapy, and cognitive services. The Center for Health Care Services and other health care agencies assist them. The concentration on rehabilitation has returned many juveniles to a productive place in society. As a result, juvenile crime has declined substantially and the juvenile dentition center has reduced its population.

Truancy is a related juvenile issue that was handled in an unfair and haphazard way. Bexar County has fifteen school districts, an unusually large number, and each had different truancy policies. In addition, they could take truancy cases either to municipal judges or to justices of the peace. Too many parents were hauled into court and assessed heavy fines when their children missed a certain number of school days. Eleven percent of students were registered as truant in 2013. These youngsters ended up with black marks on their records that could come back to haunt them later.

I worked with Mayor Julián Castro that year to create the San Antonio / Bexar County Joint Commission on Truancy to establish a uniform truancy case management program. We appointed a ten-member committee of legislators, judges, a school superintendent, and representatives of the district attorney's office, city council, and the general public. Councilman Rey Saldaña was appointed chairman. I supported Saldaña when he ran for city council in 2011 at the age of twenty-four. He is a graduate of Sanford University, where he was captain of the baseball team.

The commission issued a report in April 2014 recommending that the city and county reach a local agreement whereby all truancy cases would be filed with the presiding judge of the San Antonio Municipal Court. The city council and the Commissioners Court subsequently approved such an agreement. More importantly, each school district agreed to adopt early intervention and prevention policies to help students and parents before the young person accumulated too many absences. As a result of the new policies, the number of cases dropped from thirty-two thousand annually before the agreement to sixteen thousand cases afterward.

This commission work was a great local success and laid the foundation for a statewide program. The Bexar County model served as a blueprint for 2015 legislation that decriminalized failure to attend school. Instead, truancy became treated as a civil matter requiring measures for intervention and prevention.

## CHILD ABUSE AND NEGLECT

After I became county judge, my wife, Tracy, agreed to create a foundation and raise money to restore the historic 1892 Bexar County Courthouse. Over the years it had deteriorated, and by the time I took office in 2001 it was listed as an endangered historic structure. Because citizens view courthouses as symbols of liberty and independence, its disrepair was particularly distressing.

The largest continuously used courthouse in Texas, it is a grand structure of Romanesque Revival style, built of Texas granite and Pecos red sandstone with green clay roof tiles. The north entrance features spacious granite steps with immense granite columns and bronze lamps on each side. Two corner towers flank the front of the courthouse. I was determined to return this sacred object of justice to its monumental dignity.

As we toured the courthouse a few days after I took office, Tracy and I saw people lining the second-floor hallway. Walking through the crowd, we entered a cramped courtroom where children's cases were handled. Families with their children, representatives of social agencies, and officials with Child Protective Services (CPS) jammed the small space. Three lawyers sat at a table, one representing the parents, another representing the child, and a third from the district attorney's office, representing the state. After hearing testimony, Associate Judge Peter Sakai would decide whether to terminate parental rights. Tracy was appalled at the crowded conditions and the tense adults and children.

Tracy has a long history of supporting children. When I was mayor, she started the first Library Telethon on KENS-TV, the funds from which went to the San Antonio Library Foundation to benefit children. While serving on the local workforce commission, she chaired the committee on child care. She then founded Smart Start, which raised millions of dollars to upgrade child-care centers. She and Karen Herrmann cofounded the city's first children's museum.

Soon after our tour she met with District Judge John Specia and Sakai. Specia had hired Sakai in 1995 to assist with the rising number of abuse and neglect cases. Tracy teamed up with them to plan a state-of-the-art children's court with two child abuse courts. Betty Bueche, county facilities manager, hired a consultant to help plan the new court. The Commissioners Court approved a contract with Susan Goltsman, a leading consultant on children's courts, who sought advice from constituent groups on the court's programming and space needs.

After several months of work, a report to the Commissioners Court recommended devoting ten thousand square feet of space for two full courtrooms, an education and recreational area for children, two large conference rooms, family visitation rooms, offices for prosecutors and CPS staff, detention cells, and a drug-testing clinic. The report also recommended installing state-of-the-art technology, including video transmission.

Tracy persuaded District Clerk Reagan Greer to move his records and people from the third floor of the courthouse so the children's court complex could be built there. The Commissioners Court approved relocation and authorized hiring an architect. In 2003, as child abuse and neglect cases rose at an alarming rate, commissioners approved contracts to construct the children's court. The epidemic of child abuse continued to skyrocket in 2004, with 204 children dying from abuse and neglect in Texas, an 11 percent increase from the previous year. Bexar County saw eleven children die, compared to seven the year before.

Even while child abuse cases were rising, the Texas legislature cut funding for the Children's Health Insurance Program, or CHIP, which provides health insurance for children under eighteen in working poor families whose income is above Medicaid eligibility. Texas was ranked second-worst in the nation in providing insurance coverage for both children and adults.

The legislature also cut funding for Child Protective Services, the agency responsible for investigating child abuse cases. CPS workers initially investigate abuse and neglect cases and, based on their findings, clear the parents, or recommend criminal prosecution or termination of parental rights through a civil proceeding. The Commissioners Court offset some of the CPS shortfall by providing $2.8 million annually to cover the cost for fifty-five CPS employees.

Under the leadership of San Antonio lawmakers Senator Leticia Van de Putte and Representative Carlos Uresti, the legislature restored some funds to CPS and CHIP. But funding remained well below the level needed to address children's issues.

Because of the rise in abuse and neglect cases, in late 2004 Associate Judge Richard Garcia was transferred from the family law court to the abuse and neglect court, providing two full-time judges to handle the increased workload.

On January 14, 2005, we opened a new 12,000-square-foot children's court, 2,000 square feet more than we originally planned. Conference rooms had ample space for families to meet with their lawyers. A special room for children protected them from the trauma of court proceedings. Judges could visit with them in person, or their testimony could be transferred by video. CPS staff, the district attorney, and social service agencies had their own offices. State-of-the-art technology enabled judges to use remote videoconferencing with experts or parents. Martin Gruen, deputy director of the Center for Legal and Court Technology and the Courtroom 21 Project at the William and Mary School of Law, said at its opening that this court was now the model for the nation.

The project included not only building new court facilities but also restoring historic courtroom features such as large arched windows, historic doors, Mission-style tile floors, and marble wainscoting. In the corridor near the children's courts, workers removed ceiling tile, restored the original ceiling, and uncovered partially hidden windows.

But Tracy went one step further. She wanted the children to be comfortable as soon as they left the elevator and entered the hallway. She convinced Bruce Bugg Jr., chairman of the Tobin Endowment, to provide $100,000 for art. Artists Chuck Ramirez, Michael Velliquette, Juan Miguel Ramos, and Elizabeth Ward created thirty-one pieces for the walls along the corridor.

In addition, Tracy raised money for enhanced services. The drug-testing clinic provided weekly testing for parents who had been addicted to drugs. Perhaps not surprisingly, over 70 percent of parents of abused and neglected children are on drugs. Drug courts complemented work of the children's court because offenders who had been rehabilitated through the drug courts were then able to stabilize their families. Building the children's court cost $3.1 million, with $2.3 million in private funds raised by Tracy and the balance from county funds. Judges now made timely and informed decisions about abused and neglected children.

Altogether, Tracy has raised more than $10 million for the courthouse, including the children's court.

In 2007 Sakai succeeded Specia as an elected district judge. Associate Judge Charles Montemayor took over Sakai's abuse and neglect docket. In addition to his judicial duties, Sakai oversaw operation of the children's court, as Specia had done.

Over the years the children's court handled thousands of cases effectively. But at the same time, CPS had become so bureaucratic it was considered dysfunctional. Caseworker turnover of some 40 percent led to failure both in communication and service delivery. Instead of trying to keep families together or to make case management decisions, caseworkers simply filed them with the court to handle. The case docket became so overloaded that, as cases were delayed, the system simply fueled the income of lawyers.

Too many children were removed from their families and dumped in an overloaded foster care system. Over time, some foster children were sent to as many as thirty foster families. Then they were tossed out on the street when they turned eighteen. Like CPS, the foster care system had become dysfunctional.

In 2014 the system finally saw a ray of hope when Specia left retirement and accepted appointment as commissioner of the Texas Department of Family and Protective Services, which oversees CPS. With an ally in place, Sakai developed a plan to change the dynamics of both the children's court and CPS.

Sakai presented me and Specia with a plan to set up a data and metric system to measure the effectiveness of the children's court and CPS. The plan he proposed involved docket management and case settings to be administered by court managers and staff, much as with judicial services. CPS would be required to focus on timeliness and safety and to reward parents who were making reasonable efforts to reunify their families. Keeping families together rather than separating them became the goal.

Specia and I both signed on, and I persuaded the Commissioners Court to provide the funding. Judge Sakai appointed the court administrator: Barbara Schafer, who previously had been program director for the family drug court. Schafer had a master's degree in social work, as well as bachelor's degrees in psychology and sociology.

The program was strengthened when District Attorney Nico LaHood agreed to move his prosecutors from offices across the hall from the children's court so that six nonprofit organizations selected by Sakai could have office space there. This allowed the nonprofits to work more closely and easily with families.

Then Sakai created an early intervention program to focus on mothers with infants or toddlers ages three and under where CPS already had intervened. The program focuses on mental health needs of the mother, helping her bond with her child.

Tracy teamed up with Dennis Noll, president and CEO of the San Antonio Area Foundation, to raise funds from the Santikos Foundation, the Baptist Health Foundation, and Temple Beth-El. More than $1 million was raised for the program, which was scheduled to start in late 2016.

At the same time, as soon as he was elected, LaHood and his office stepped up vigorous prosecution of criminal child abuse cases. In 2015, his first year, he conducted nearly twice as many trials as the year before. He had a 70 percent conviction rate, compared to 54 percent the year before. The average conviction rate statewide is 55 percent.

With the state-of-the-art children's court, the successful effort to reunify families, the intervention program to focus on children ages three years and younger, nonprofit organizations' close proximity to the court, and LaHood's prosecution of criminal abuse cases, this county is on the right path to save children.

## JUSTICE DELAYED

At the same time that we addressed therapeutic justice, child abuse and neglect cases, and juvenile justice, we also took steps to create a more efficient criminal justice system, because justice delayed is justice denied. The Commissioners Court does not have authority to demand greater efficiency from elected judges, sheriff, district attorney, or county and district clerks. But we do have budget authority and the right to monitor the criminal justice system and report our findings to the voters. Using these tools, we took steps to bring some coherence and efficiency to the justice system.

In 2003 the Commissioners Court reached an agreement with the city, the judges, and the sheriff to create a central magistration center. We combined the booking staffs of the sheriff's office, city municipal judges, pretrial release staff, assistant district attorneys, and bail bondsmen into the central magistrate division at the Frank D. Wing Municipal Court Building. At a facility that is unique in the state, the accused are booked, and a magistrate judge decides whether to set bail or incarcerate them.

In the first year of operation, 2,450 accused were processed. Almost half of them, 1,026, made bond and were released. On average, 30 fewer went to jail each day. We saved $1 million in the first full year.

In addition to the magistration center, the Commissioners Court continued to fund a jail court we had previously implemented. A visiting judge operates on the first floor of the jail to review nonviolent misdemeanor and minor felony cases of inmates for possible release. The impact of central magistration in bonding out the nonviolent accused before transferring them to jail reduced the jail court work by over 50 percent, from a high of 12,658 cases to 6,155 as of 2016.

We took another step forward four years later when the Commissioners Court budgeted funds for county magistrates to replace municipal judges who were serving as magistrates. District judges appoint the county magistrates, subject to approval by the Commissioners Court. This arrangement gave the Commissioners Court veto power on any proposed judge who did not believe in setting reasonable bail or be willing to divert nonviolent offenders to treatment for drug abuse and mental problems.

In 2005 the Commissioners Court took a major step forward in reforming the judicial system when we created the criminal justice planning and coordination department. It was charged with monitoring the size of the jail population, the number of personal recognizance bonds issued, and the cost of indigent defense. The crime laboratory, morgue, and central magistrate office were put under its jurisdiction.

In the same year we created the public defender's office to represent indigent defendants on appeal with the idea that, if this step proved successful, we would expand the scope of the office.

While our criminal justice planning and coordination department had some success, the Commissioners Court was not making headway in encouraging judges to run more efficient courts. Local judges took, on average, three times longer to dispose of criminal cases than the American Bar Association recommended. Thus 60 percent of county jail inmates were awaiting trial. Several studies have shown the longer nonviolent people sit in jail, the more likely they are to be influenced by dangerous criminals.

Part of the judicial problem is that Texas has an extremely poor system for selecting judges. We are one of only eight states still selecting judges through partisan elections. This system, which requires judges to run both in a primary and then in a general election, is both costly for judicial candidates and confusing for the public.

Sixty-four judges are elected in Bexar County for four-year terms. Voters select judges for the Fourth Court of Appeals, district and county courts, probate courts, and juvenile courts, and justices of the peace. Every two years, Bexar County has as many as seventy or eighty judicial candidates running for thirty-eight posts in Republican and Democratic primaries. Party activists think their party's strength is partially determined by the number of judges they elect. So they work hard to elect their nominees, regardless of whether they are qualified. Each party encourages their constituents to "pull the lever," meaning with one push of the computer button you vote for every nominee your party is fielding.

The most popular political party at that time elects most of its nominees. In presidential election years, Democrats often prevail. In years when governors are elected, fewer people vote, and Republicans win. The state has lost numerous good judges simply because they were running in the wrong election cycle.

As a result of running in both a primary and a general election, judicial candidates must raise huge sums of money from special interest groups. In the case of criminal court judges, defense attorneys—the only ones deeply interested in results—provide the financing. This puts judges in a difficult position when they decide who gets appointed to defend indigent defendants and what expenses they will be allowed.

The problem is particularly serious when judges rule on numerous requests by defense attorneys to delay cases. The longer a case is deferred, the more difficult it is to obtain a conviction. The memories of witnesses fade, and evidence disappears. Thus defense attorneys make repeated requests for delays. Some defendants are in jail for more than three years awaiting trial.

In assigning cases, judges are supposed to follow the wheel, a fixed rotating list of criminal defense attorneys. In 2010 research found that some judges did not follow the wheel, and hundreds of defense attorneys were appointed whose names were not on the wheel. Only a small number of the 645 attorneys on the wheel were getting the business.

I have testified at judicial hearings in the Texas House to change the way the state selects judges and have supported legislation requiring that judicial candidates run in nonpartisan elections. Such elections would be less costly because they would require one election rather than both a primary and general election. Voters would be less confused because they could focus on the candidates' merits rather than their party affiliation. Obviously, the legislature has not been swayed. But in 2017 the legislature did take a step forward. Beginning in the 2020 election, straight party voting will not be available. People will have to make independent choices and judge candidates on their merits, not just party affiliation.

So judges perform their duties in a faulty electoral criminal justice system not of their making. The county has many good judges, as evidenced by their willingness to administer therapeutic justice through the innovative specialty courts. I wanted to reform and streamline the criminal justice system to recognize the good work that several judges were doing.

In 2009 we finally found someone to run the criminal justice planning and coordination department who had both judicial knowledge and the sharp teeth to chew through the insulated criminal justice system. That person was Judge Timothy Johnson, who had just retired and had demonstrated the ability to run an efficient court. Most important, he was not influenced by donations from criminal defense attorneys.

Obviously, many defense lawyers and judges opposed his appointment. They knew he had the knowledge to shake up the system. In a contentious court session, we voted 3–2 to hire him.

Once on board, he focused on a vigorous multilevel program

to bring efficiency to the criminal justice system. We restructured the department, renaming it the judicial services division. The Commissioners Court authorized additional staff for Johnson to begin a very controversial program: he would judge the judges. Only someone of his caliber could administer a fair, impartial ranking of judges.

He set up a system to measure the efficiency of each judge, ranking each on the number of cases handled and the time taken to dispose of them. He presented quarterly reports to the Commissioners Court on the rankings, which were made available to the San Antonio Bar Association and the public. This provided voters a report card on how well each judge ran his or her court in comparison to the others.

No judge wanted to be ranked toward the bottom. After a few slacker judges were defeated, the remaining judges began to pick up their feet and work harder. Over the years, the gap narrowed between best and worst judges, taking them all to a higher level. Judges worked longer hours and reset fewer cases. The system began to move more efficiently.

Once the program was firmly in place, Johnson decided to retire, but he left behind a team of experts who developed a working relationship with the judges and helped them streamline their court operations.

Mike Lozito was hired as his successor in spring 2012. He had worked for the Texas Department of Criminal Justice for twenty-eight years, then joined the county as judicial support services manager in 2010.

Lozito began adding programs to strengthen the department, creating a pretrial diversion program for first-time youth offenders. More than 770 youth were placed in the program.

He hired two additional forensic technicians to speed up the results of drug tests, providing results within twenty days, instead of the previous sixty days. This shortened the time offenders spent in jail. Lozito also worked to strengthen and expand the county's success with the initial appearance, or probable cause hearing, overseen by a magistrate.

In 2014 we took a major step at the central magistrate facility to address the mental health issues of people who had been arrested. County Manager David Smith hired Gilbert Gonzalez, a former Center for Health Care Services executive, to be the director of the Bexar County Mental Health Department, a division of the judicial services division.

He was charged with establishing a mental health review for arrested people. If the initial screening revealed any mental health problems, clinicians would provide full assessments and recommend to the magistrates whether the people should be diverted to a treatment center. The Commissioners Court provided funding to make clinicians available sixteen hours a day, seven days a week, to interview people with mental health issues.

That same year we hired Michael Young as chief public defender. Young, who had an economics degree and a law degree, had been a prosecutor, a private criminal defense lawyer, and an assistant federal public defender. We also authorized three new positions and expanded the role of the public defender's office.

Some of Young's staff were assigned to probable cause hearings, working with assistant district attorneys to review reports from clinicians and to make recommendations to the magistrates. In 2015 magistrates diverted 194 individuals to treatment programs. In early 2016, they were on track to divert 420 for the year.

After LaHood was elected district attorney in 2014, he took steps to reform his office. He presented to the Commissioners Court a plan to create a decentralized system that allowed assistant district attorneys to make more decisions about pleas, replacing a hierarchical system that delayed decision-making. The commissioners increased his budget by $1.3 million, and within a few months the jail population decreased.

In May 2016 we opened a reentry services center to assist inmates reentering society. Each year, thousands of men and women in Bexar County are released from state jails and prisons and from federal prisons. Many are repeat offenders. More than 56 percent are rearrested within first year, and 76.6 percent are rearrested within five years. With a consolidated center, we hoped to break the cycle.

We housed the reentry center in a large building two blocks from the jail that we had purchased. We built office space, plus conference rooms and meeting rooms for families and for representatives of social services agencies and the faith-based community. The conference space was open for uses such as Alcoholics Anonymous meetings and literacy classes. The facility included an electronic library, part of BiblioTech, the county's electronic library.

Lozito appointed Debra Jordan, who had more than thirty-five years of experience as deputy jail administrator, as the reentry program manager. She would coordinate the work of sixty-five agencies to help inmates reenter society after they had served their time. Services offered included employment, education, housing, substance abuse, and social services.

While the faith-based community is important to the reentry center, they also play a key role in helping many other people with mental illness. In 2016 Doug Beach and the Reverend Carol Morehead visited with me about organizing a Pathways to Hope Conference. I agreed that the county would support them. I spoke at the opening of the two-day conference in August at the Tobin Center, attended by more than 1,400 church leaders. Many of the churches agreed to organized mental health ministries. The conference was so successful that we decided to have annual sessions. We held the next one in August 2017.

We also opened a videoconferencing center for visitors to communicate with jail inmates. We located it in the same building as the reentry center. Family members who came to video-visit with their loved ones could go to the reentry center to help prepare for their release.

Across a parking lot from the reentry center, the Commissioners Court converted a warehouse into a 140-bed work-release center to house inmates whose good conduct allowed them to work during the day. This gave them the ability to earn money for their families while serving time.

While we have successfully implemented therapeutic justice over the last fifteen years, some offenders with mental health and drug abuse issues who do pose a threat to society must remain in jail. Although we have reduced mentally ill and drug-dependent inmates from a high of 40 percent of the population, still some 20 percent have mental and drug abuse issues.

As of 2016, some 125 University Hospital medical personnel serve incarcerated inmates around the clock. That includes 25 full-time employees who care for inmates with mental problems. In 2015 they treated some 1,300 inmates with mental problems. Rather than transport inmates to University Hospital, the county built a twenty-six-bed clinical observation unit at the jail.

In 2016 the Commissioners Court took a major step forward in improving the medical services in our jail and repositioning the location of central magistration. We funded the remodeling of the women's area to include additional medical beds, as well as obstetrical, detox, and mental health units.

We decommissioned some 1,000 jail beds and leased them to GEO, a private correctional company, to house federal prisoners. This enabled us to demolish our 680-bed Laredo Street detention center, located in the center of the city, which had been leased to GEO. Removing the ugly old detention center would enable us to market our downtown property to a developer.

In place of the decommissioned jail beds, the court provided funding to build a five-story facility with 864 beds to replace jail space that we had leased to GEO. The building, which will connect to the main jail, will include classrooms, enhanced mental health and medical initiatives, and expanded programs to better prepare inmates for release from jail.

The bottom floor will include an intake and assessment center. We will be able to hold up to three hundred people who have been arrested for up to seventy-two hours, enabling them to be bonded or possibly sent to treatment rather than incarcerated. In the old city building, they could be held only eighteen hours, requiring that they be transported to the jail before their outcomes could be determined. We expect the center to open in 2018.

## A NEW DRUG CRISIS: OPIOID AND SYNTHETIC CANNABINOIDS

The year 2017 put additional pressure on the judiciary, jail population, and therapeutic justice. Dangerous drugs—heroin and prescription opiates along with synthetic cannabinoids—infiltrated society and played a large role in driving up crime and creating a public health crisis. The nationwide opioid epidemic also caused a public health and public safety crisis in San Antonio.

Synthetic cannabinoids are a class of chemicals that bind to cannabinoids through the spraying and soaking of marijuana plants. The combinations of chemicals can prove to be very dangerous, causing agitation, psychoses, hallucination, and other dangerous reactions. They can even lead to death. They are sold under such names as K-2 and Black Mamba.

Opioids are synthetic derivatives of opium, such as Vicodin, oxycontin, hydrocodone, carfentanil, and fentanyl. Fentanyl is thirty to fifty times more potent than heroin, a natural derivative from opium. Sixty-two thousand Americans died from drug overdoses in 2016, and two-thirds of those died from opioids.

The pharmaceutical industry has added to the problem. Legal opioid prescriptions have quadrupled since 1999, with more than 650,000 such prescriptions dispensed daily. In 2016 more than 10 million Americans reported nonmedical abuse of prescription opioids. Chronic misuse of opioids increases risk for infection, HIV, and hepatitis and is the leading cause of accidental death. The opioid epidemic is blamed for more common postpartum deaths and higher incidence of respiratory and neurological diseases in infants.

Partly as a result of the increase in more dangerous drugs, violent crime, including murders, went up in 2016. In early 2017 the police and sheriff's department created a Violent Crime Task Force. At the same time, they started a warrant roundup of nonviolent offenders. Bookings at our jail went up 11 percent in the first six months of 2017. The Commissioners Court had to authorize $2.5 million in overtime pay for deputies. We also made arrangements with Karnes County to take some prisoners on a temporary basis.

In April 2017 the Commissioners Court approved funding for a felony impact court to speed up the hearing process. Former Judge Laura Parker was appointed and immediately began to increase the number of dispositions. In July I met with both the District and County Court at Law Judges to put in place extra court hearings. We are also expanding the use of personal recognizance bonds for nonviolent offenders and the use of GPS.

Recognizing that we need a communitywide action plan to combat this growing drug threat to the health and safety of our community, on June 20 the Commissioners Court approved the creation of a task force to explore various treatment programs, law enforcement policies, and regulations to curtain distribution of these dangerous drugs. Newly elected Mayor Ron Nirenberg agreed to expand it into a city-county task force. University Hospital Chief Medical Officer Bryan Alsip and Metro Public Health Director Dr. Colleen Bridger agreed to cochair the effort. The task force included law enforcement officials, health care providers, pharmacies, first responders, social services agencies, and school districts. My chief of staff, T. J. Mayes, also agreed to staff the task force. Mayes is an attorney and was chief of staff for Ron Nirenberg when he was a councilman.

The task force will address the following topics: training law enforcement officials to use overdose reversal drugs; guidelines for health care providers on how to properly prescribe drugs; policies to decrease the availability of prescribed opioids; treatment best practices; hospital guidelines that seek alternatives to opioid treatment; medical school training addressing the dangers of opioids; the marketing of opioids by the pharmaceutical industry;

more aggressive postal inspections of packages; and congressional action to halt dark web distribution.

In 2018 the reform of our criminal justice system is under additional challenges to treat drug addiction. More treatment programs will have to be created. With new programs, we will work our way through this roundup of offenders and should be able to stabilize our jail population, bringing us back to 2016 levels, which averaged about 3,600 inmates.

Most important, we will need to stick our core philosophy: punish the bad people, help cure the nonviolent offender, and run the criminal system efficiently. Specialty courts—drug, mental health, veterans, DWI, and Esperanza—have been successful in treating nonviolent offenders. The restorative center, which the Center for Health Care Services implemented to include both mental health crisis care and a detoxification program, has diverted thousands of offenders from jail. Haven for Hope has helped prevent many homeless people from entering a life of crime. Treatment programs within the jail have helped numerous inmates. University Hospital's medical staff have stabilized many patients who experience mental health issues.

The office of public defender has become a center for best practices. We are now able to access the effectiveness and efficiency of private defense lawyers assigned to the indigent. The public defender's office has played a huge role in advocating before magistrates the need to refer many arrested people for treatment. We now have twelve public defender lawyers.

Our new reentry center is providing an array of services to help former inmates transition back into society and avoid becoming repeat offenders. The magistration center has streamlined the operation of the entry point for offenders. Our new facility will be a substantial improvement. Treatment of juveniles at the detention center and correctional facility has enabled young people to turn their lives around. Thanks to changes in truancy procedures, fewer parents and young people are hauled to court. The children's court has succeeded in holding families together rather than removing the child from the family.

Greater efficiency in managing court dockets will continue to be improved. The judicial support division's ranking of courts has encouraged judges to implement best practices.

With public support, we will overcome this drug crisis. Our criminal justice system will meet the challenges along with the numerous organizations that seek to help the mentally ill and those with drug addiction problems.

# FIVE

## A New Tech Ecosystem

WHEN I WAS TWENTY-EIGHT years old and two years out of St. Mary's School of Law, I went to the opening day of HemisFair '68, whose theme was "Confluence of Civilizations in the Americas." The World's Fair woke up this sleepy town and set the stage for the growth of tourism. Located on ninety-six acres east of downtown, it drew millions to celebrate San Antonio's 250th anniversary. I remember walking among the forty-five pavilions representing more than thirty nations and fifteen corporations, passing underneath the elevated monorail, and meandering past dozens of food booths as singers and dancers performed.

It was a grand time for San Antonio, but looking back I recognize that the city should not have put all its resources into the World's Fair. It should have paid attention to a more significant event taking place across town. On July 31, 1968, two former NASA engineers, Phil Ray and Gus Roche, founded Computer Terminal Corporation. Former Frost Bank president Joe Frost Jr. financially backed them and insisted that they locate in San Antonio.

The firm developed computer terminals to replace noisy teletype machines that connected to large mainframe computers. The following year, in 1969, they built a production facility off IH-10 near Wurzbach Road. As they broke ground, the virtual world of the internet was coming to life. ARPANET, a network run on packet switching, connected computers at Stanford University and UCLA.

Victor Poor, the engineer in charge of research, drew up specs for an eight-bit processor and an "intelligent terminal" allowing offline data entry and independent data processing. In 1970 the company introduced a computer terminal and named the model Datapoint 2200. The terminal was so popular that the owners changed their corporate name to Datapoint Corporation. At $13,000 each, the terminal was too expensive for the average person or small business, but larger businesses with mainframes scooped it up.

Datapoint was a creative company, driving innovations such as wireless extended-range networking and videoconferencing over a network. It created the metal oxide silicon computer chip and desktop computer networks. It also produced a laser printer and the Resource Management System, or RMS. In short, Datapoint was on top of the tech world, and so was San Antonio.

From 1973 to 1981 Datapoint sales increased 40 percent annually. By 1981 it was a Fortune 500 company with sales of $450 million. San Antonio employees numbered more than 3,000, and the company had a total of 8,900 employees worldwide. In addition to the production plant, Datapoint leased thirty-five buildings in San Antonio. Several of them, once home to its workforce, still stand on Datapoint Drive between Wurzbach and Fredericksburg Road.

In 1981 a troubling sign occurred when IBM introduced a PC for as little as $1,500. Pricing at Datapoint for a similar computer was $8,725. While IBM received credit for developing the first personal computer, the first patent was issued for the Datapoint 2200. Today every personal computer can be traced back to that model.

As competition grew and its products aged, Datapoint covered up its problems by booking sales for orders it had not received. The *Wall Street Journal* broke the story. The wheels started to come off in the third quarter of 1982 when the company posted its first quarterly loss after thirty-nine straight quarterly profits. Five key executives left the company, 250 employees were laid off, and plans for a $50 million San Antonio headquarters complex were abandoned.

By 1985 Datapoint was struggling to stay alive when investor Asher B. Edelman took control of the company and became chairman. Mayor Henry Cisneros vowed to do everything he could to keep the company in San Antonio. Two years later Edelman laid off 35 percent of Datapoint's corporate staff. A year after that he took the company private in an attempt to achieve greater stability away from the public eye.

As Datapoint continued to struggle with losses and layoffs, Edelman decided in 1990 to move its headquarters to Paris. Datapoint was by then down to 278 manufacturing employees in San Antonio. By 2002 only 26 employees remained, and the last trace of the company was vanishing quickly.

After Datapoint failed, San Antonio fell off the tech shelf, and communities like Austin, San Francisco, and Silicon Valley took off like skyrockets. Because San Antonio relied strictly on Datapoint and did not foster a diversified technology industry, it lost a great opportunity to build a thriving tech community. Had the city paid more attention to Datapoint, it could have built an ecosystem to foster other high-tech firms. The city and community leaders' lack of foresight was a lesson we would later remember.

## THE MILITARY, NSA, AND CYBERSECURITY

While Datapoint remained barely breathing in the 1990s, a series of important decisions at the federal level regarding military missions and the National Security Agency had tech implications for San Antonio. During the decision-making process, community leaders began to work with the military and NSA to foster major tech initiatives for San Antonio that included cybersecurity, aerospace, and biomedical.

Between 1995 and 2005, recommendations of the Defense Base Realignment and Closure Commission, known as BRAC, created a major upheaval at our five local military bases—Lackland, Brooks, Kelly, Randolph, and Fort Sam Houston. As mayor and later as county judge, I participated in four BRAC processes that changed the face of the local military and had a huge impact on the evolution of technology in San Antonio.

Through the first two BRAC phases, our community successfully defended its bases. That changed in the 1995 BRAC round. In July of that year, two months after I had completed two terms as mayor, BRAC announced it was recommending to Congress the closure of Kelly Air Force Base, a major air logistics center that, at its height, had employed twenty-five thousand people.

I heard the radio announcement about the closure as I sat in my office at Sun Harvest Natural Foods headquarters. This was heartbreaking because Kelly had a special meaning to all of us who grew up in San Antonio. We all had close friends or relatives who had worked at Kelly. My dad had worked there during World War II. The base also provided opportunities for numerous

Latino families who made their way into the middle class through the thousands of civilian jobs that Kelly offered.

Under the leadership of my successor, Mayor Bill Thornton, the city aggressively lobbied President Bill Clinton to delay the closing for five years. The president granted the extension, giving our community time to plan for Kelly's privatization. On July 13, 2001, some five years after the announcement of Kelly's closing and two months after I became county judge, I joined Howard Peak, another former mayor, at Kelly Air Force Base for an official ceremony to turn the base over to the city. We sat under a large oak tree on the lawn of the base commander's headquarters. Running my hands over the gnarled trunk, I guessed that it was probably older than the eighty-five-year-old air base. On that day, Kelly reached the end of its life as an Air Force logistics center, but the life of the tree would continue.

As more than twenty television cameras focused on the sweating dignitaries, Peak and I enjoyed the shade of the tree, and I told him, "Good day to be an ex-mayor." He smiled. As the ceremony ended, Mayor Ed Garza accepted an encased flag and the "base key." Then a C-5 Galaxy cargo plane, the major aircraft maintained at Kelly, flew over, followed by four F-16 Fighting Falcon jets.

Because of the five-year transition to the private sector, San Antonio had time to put together an effective redevelopment program. After gaining control of the base, the city created an incentive program, which got off to a running start when Boeing and Lockheed Martin became the first two large companies to locate at Kelly. They, along with six local aerospace companies, created an Aerospace Academy in a partnership with the Alamo Community College District. High school juniors and seniors were eligible for the program, which incorporated aerospace-related training and college academic courses leading to great-paying technology jobs.

One year later, on July 22, 2002, I was again with Peak, this time at Brooks Air Force Base. Tucked away in the shade of Hangar 9, a long rectangular platform held Air Force and local officials, including me. We watched as the early morning sun peeked from behind the roving clouds and shone down on the glistering foreheads of the crowd facing Hangar 9, the last remaining World War II hangar in the United States. As we sat in the shade and members of the crowd sat in the sun shading their faces with cardboard hand fans, I said to Peak, "This is a good day to be a public official."

On the platform was the podium that President John F. Kennedy had spoken from on November 21, 1963, when he dedicated the School of Aerospace Medicine. Only about an hour before that speech, I had stood on the curb at our family building material company on Roosevelt Avenue while Kennedy and his wife, Jacqueline, rode by in a convertible waving to us. I had entered St. Mary's University law school that fall and was excited to see the forty-six-year-old president who had aroused such hopes for my generation. The following day, President Kennedy was killed in Dallas, dimming those hopes and dreams.

Behind the audience was a memorial park with the grave of Cadet Sidney J. Brooks Jr., for whom the base was named. He had died in 1917, the first San Antonio native killed in service related to World War I.

Sad as the reminders were that day, we were celebrating a new life for Brooks Air Force Base. For the first time in history, an operating military base was forming a partnership with a city. It would become known as Brooks City-Base. The partnership came about as the city's attempt to help prevent the closure of Brooks.

The city council created a public corporation and appointed an eleven-member board, with Peak as chairman.

Two years later, on July 15, 2004, Peak, Garza, and I struck a deal with John Feik, CEO of DPT Laboratories, to build a research and production center on the base. The company broke ground the next year for a 254,000-square-foot building to house 175 workers in well-paid jobs researching and producing pharmaceutical drugs.

With the privatization of Kelly and partial privatization of Brooks, the city faced another round of base closures in 2005. We created a task force and retained retired Air Force Brigadier General John Jernigan to prepare for that BRAC round. He led the effort to assess our current military missions to determine which ones might be vulnerable.

On May 13, 2005, the Department of Defense made its recommendations to the BRAC commission, the first step in the process. That morning our local task force gathered at eight o'clock in the city council's conference room to listen to the public announcement. Right before that announcement, Representative Lamar Smith faxed us the list of the proposed closures and mission realignments. As we added up the plus and minuses, we quickly realized that we had gained a lot of new jobs. A few minutes later, Senator John Cornyn called. Over the speakerphone, I asked him, "Our list shows that we will have a net increase of about 3,100 jobs. Did your staff review the list?"

"Yes, they did," he replied. "And our numbers are the same."

On the downside, the Defense Department recommended to the nine-member BRAC commission that the military missions at Brooks City-Base be relocated and the base be closed. Some personnel would be moved to Wright-Patterson Air Force Base in Ohio; others would be reassigned to other local bases in San Antonio. We were prepared for the closure because of the move toward to privatization that began in 2002 with the creation of Brooks City-Base partnership between the city and the military.

Most important was a recommendation that the Army medical training mission at Fort Sam Houston should be expanded to include all branches of the military. It would become a center of medical excellence, offering numerous tech-related jobs. Over the next five years more than $2 billion would be invested for expansion of Brooke Army Medical Center and for other base upgrades. One important component of the medical center was the Army Institute of Surgical Research, the Defense Department's only research facility focusing on advanced treatment of severely wounded service members.

While we were happy with the net new jobs, we fought to keep one Brooks mission that was headed to Ohio: the eight-hundred-employee Cryptologic Systems Group. We had to win this battle because we were simultaneously working to bring a center of the National Security Agency here, and the Cryptologic Systems Group was important to its mission.

The NSA is the nation's cryptology and communications monitoring service, which gathers and analyzes foreign intelligence. Its headquarters lie about ten miles from Washington, DC, at Fort Meade, where approximately thirty thousand people work. For several years we had tried unsuccessfully to convince its leadership to open a site in San Antonio. The 9/11 terrorist attacks changed the NSA's thinking, and they began planning to disperse some of the Fort Meade operations. Eventually those plans included opening four regional centers.

San Antonio was a natural location for one of them. More

than 2,300 people worked in Air Force intelligence at Lackland Air Force Base. Eight hundred people worked in the Cryptologic Systems Group. CPS Energy provided reliable electrical power, and the city had a large fiber-optic technology network. In addition, a former Sony microchip manufacturing plant at Loop 410 and Military Drive was just the type of site a center needed.

All our work paid off in April 2005 when NSA announced that it would open a regional headquarters, locating 1,500 employees at the former Sony plant. These were high-paying jobs. Sixty percent of its employees had advanced degrees. The NSA is the nation's largest employer of mathematicians.

Because NSA worked closely with the Air Force's Cryptologic Systems Group, we needed help from them to turn around the decision to move the group to Ohio. While we were in the nation's capital for the annual chambers of commerce trip, on June 10, 2005, Chamber Chairman John Montford, Chamber President Joe Krier, John Dickson, CEO of the Denim Group, a cybersecurity firm, and I quietly slipped away early one morning for a visit to NSA headquarters at Fort Meade.

We drove through two security checkpoints as we approached the massive building complex and a third as we entered the building for a meeting with ten NSA officials. After a briefing, lunch, and discussion of issues associated with the move to San Antonio, they told us how important it was for the Cryptologic Systems Group to remain in San Antonio. We asked them to join our effort by asking the BRAC commission to leave the group in San Antonio. They agreed to help.

Viewing a model of the regional center on a large table, I commented, "That's a lot of parking spaces."

One of the NSA officials said, "Count them." When we had

counted 4,500 parking spaces, we realized that the original number of 1,500 employees would grow over time.

The BRAC commission on August 5, 2005, voted to accept the Department of Defense recommendations with two exceptions. They voted to leave the Cryptologic Systems Group in San Antonio and moved 275 jobs in directed energy research to Fort Sam Houston. By saving the two missions, we had a net increase in jobs of 4,200 instead of 3,100.

We were now in high cotton. The aerospace companies that were located at Kelly gave us a leg up on technology associated with their firms. The medical mission at Fort Sam complemented the local healthcare industry and added technology jobs. More important, the series of decisions by the BRAC commission and NSA led San Antonio to become the major center for cybersecurity outside of Fort Meade.

The city later benefited again when the Air Force consolidated its cyberspace combat and support forces into the Twenty-Fourth Air Force, with a cyberwarfare mission and fourteen thousand airmen in its workforce. In May 2009, Air Force officials announced that land connected to Port San Antonio, formerly Kelly Air Force Base, would become the site of headquarters for the Twenty-Fourth Air Force.

Another major step came five years later: on September 29, 2014, the Air Force established the Twenty-Fifth Air Force to provide intelligence, surveillance, and reconnaissance capabilities, including cyber and geospatial forces. The Twenty-Fifth also included the eight hundred personnel in the Cryptologic System Group, which played a major role in the decision to locate its headquarters at Lackland Air Force Base.

The Twenty-Fourth and Twenty-Fifth Air Force Commands,

along with the NSA, have made San Antonio the epicenter for cybersecurity outside Washington, DC. The three are integrated to both defend and attack computer systems worldwide. Today some 6,500 military and civilian cyber workers are in San Antonio. We believe that somewhere between 3,000 and 4,000 employees work at NSA.

The combination of BRAC decisions and the NSA decision to locate in San Antonio led to a dramatic growth in tech jobs in cybersecurity, biomedicine, and aerospace. Most important, the Twenty-Fourth and Twenty-Fifth Air Force Commands and NSA have led to the creation of numerous private cybersecurity firms that would become the cornerstone of our continuing efforts to foster a tech industry in San Antonio. We will return to this topic below.

### SATAI

When we began our initial work with the military and NSA to bring in tech jobs, a few local tech entrepreneurs began discussing how they could revive and diversify San Antonio's private sector technology industry. In 1997 David Spencer, founder of OnBoard Software, led an effort to form Technology Advocates of San Antonio (TASA).

At the time, as chairman of the Greater San Antonio Chamber of Commerce, I called Spencer to thank him for organizing TASA. "We used to bitch and moan about the graybeards in San Antonio's business leadership who did not understand the economic potential of high tech and how to grow it," he said. "So we decided to do something about it."

"Well, I am one of the chamber graybeards," I replied. "I was here when Datapoint started in 1968 and then watched it go down in the 1990s. I hope you guys can get the industry going."

"We will make a comeback," he promised.

TASA persuaded the city council to fund a study to identify tech sectors with a potential for growth. The study identified four high-tech clusters: biosciences, information technology, telecommunications, and aerospace. The study also recommended forming a nonprofit group to foster the tech industry's development.

Southwest Research Institute had numerous research programs under way that cut across the four sectors identified by the study. Founded in 1947 by oilman and explorer Tom Slick Jr., it had grown into one of the largest independent, nonprofit, applied research and development organizations in the United States. Located on 1,200 acres off Loop 410 and Culebra Road, the institute included 2 million square feet of laboratories, test facilities, workshops, and office space. More than 2,700 employees worked in applied physics, automation and data systems, defense and intelligent solutions, and space technology, as well as chemistry, geosciences, and mechanical engineering. The institute would prove to be the foundation for the high-tech clusters.

In April 2001 the city council appropriated $1 million to fund the San Antonio Technology Accelerator Initiative (SATAI). A thirty-two-member board, made up of leaders from local academic and research institutions and successful tech entrepreneurs such as Elaine Mendoza, CEO of Conceptual MindWorks; G. P. Singh, founder and CEO of Karta Technologies; David Heard, chief marketing director for SecureLogix; Nancy Kudla, cofounder and CEO for dNovus; John Dickson, CEO of the Denim Group; John Feik, CEO of DPT Laboratories; and Spencer led the effort.

After I became county judge the following month, Spencer called and said, "The board of SATAI wants you to join me as cochair. You chaired the greater chamber, and we need a link to the general business community." I told him to count me in.

The organization got off to a rocky start. A search firm recommended that SATAI hire Tony Fisher as president, and a SATAI board subcommittee recommended him. Fisher was a New Yorker with an impressive résumé.

After my wife Tracy and I had dinner with Fisher and Spencer, we told Spencer we did not think the New Yorker was the right person to lead SATAI. "His answers were evasive. In fact, some were incoherent," I said. Tracy added, "He never made eye contact. I have a very bad feeling about him."

"I don't feel good about him either," Spencer said, "but I need to support the search committee. It has approved his recommendation."

"Well, it's up to the executive committee to hire him," I said. "I'm not a member."

"Do me a personal favor and go along with its recommendation," Spencer said.

"Okay. I may be wrong."

Just a few days after Fisher was hired, someone sent a newspaper article from his hometown of Albany, New York, with facts contradicting information in his application. Spencer paid for the law firm of Haynes and Boone to investigate.

On February 26, 2002, at the Institute of Texan Cultures, Spencer and I called a meeting of the full board to give Fisher a hearing. Our strange set of bylaws required a vote of the entire board, not just the executive committee, to fire the president. I had agreed to chair the meeting.

As we waited to begin, I said to Fisher, "I have seen the report. I would resign if I were you. I believe I can get the board to give you six months of severance."

"No," he said. "I want a full hearing."

After our law firm presented its findings, followed by a presentation by Fisher and his attorney, we excused them and began deliberations. The evidence was overwhelming. Fisher claimed to be a member of the New York State Bar Association, but the bar had no record that he was licensed to practice law. He claimed to be president of National Finance Corporation. A bankruptcy judge had ruled that Fisher never had been officially appointed president or CEO and placed the corporation into Chapter 7 liquidation.

The day was difficult, because volunteers hate controversy and certainly do not want to vote to fire someone. But after a long debate, the board voted 28–0, with four abstentions, to fire Fisher.

After the meeting, Spencer told me, "You saved SATAI. You got it off the operating table."

"David, you guys have the burden of being brilliant but not living long enough to recognize a con man," I said. "This was a wonderful lesson for you."

We had to reestablish integrity in the community quickly by finding an executive who would give us instant credibility. Spencer found the man. He persuaded Richard Love, former CEO of Ilex Oncology, to take the job temporarily. Love had taken the San Antonio–based company from a million-dollar to a billion-dollar capitalization. He probably was the only local person who could have given SATAI instant credibility.

Love took the reins and quietly got SATAI on the right track, leading the board to develop a clearer focus for the organization.

He concentrated on raising capital to help expand and develop high-tech companies. He also led a search committee that recommended Randy Goldsmith, former president of the Oklahoma Alliance for Manufacturing, as president. After Goldsmith accepted the position on October 15, 2002, he focused on matching high-tech entrepreneurs and investors. SATAI held its first South Texas Funding Forum, which eventually became an annual event. Several hundred entrepreneurs and financial investors who attended the forum learned of opportunities in areas such as high-speed connectivity, voice/handwriting programming, high-quality video, and high-resolution flat-screens.

To expand and complement the military presence in cybersecurity, SATAI worked with UTSA in 2001 to establish the Center for Infrastructure Assurance and Security, which collaborates with academia, industry, and government in providing research and educational support and training in internet and computer security.

By 2014 UTSA had grown its program to include some 1,000 undergraduates in cybersecurity and related fields and 230 students in graduate courses in cybersecurity. In a 2014 Hewlett Packard survey, UTSA was named number one in the world for cybersecurity education and outreach by Ponemon Institute.

While military missions were expanding locally, SATAI assisted several high-tech companies in gaining military contracts. The military quadrupled the money spent through outsourcing from 2000 to 2005. High-tech firms such as Karta Technologies, Vecna Technologies, ASM Research, CACI, Force 3, OnBoard Software, and Frontline Systems benefited from increased military spending. SATAI also raised capital for several private computer security firms including Novus Technology Solutions, Kratos

SecureInfo, and SecureLogix. By 2003 SATAI had assisted several high-tech firms in obtaining more than $40 million in capital.

SATAI also supported efforts by UTSA to expand its research programs in biotechnology. Spencer gave $1 million to these research programs. On February 10, 2006, UTSA announced that it would build an $83 million, 227,000-square-foot Biotechnology, Sciences, and Engineering Building. Mark G. Yudof, chancellor of the UT System, told the assembled crowd, "UTSA can now draw the best scientists and researchers with this new facility and state-of-the-art equipment. You can now apply the magic of science and mathematics to the dreams of making UTSA a premier research institution."

The building design included seventy laboratories for teaching and research in the areas of biomechanics, photonics, bioelectromechanical systems, plant biotechnology, bacterial pathogenesis, and advanced implant materials and systems. Laboratory work would complement research on emerging infectious diseases taking place in the 22,000-square-foot Margaret Batts Tobin Laboratory Building that opened in 2005. Research in these two buildings helped foster the San Antonio Life Sciences Institute, a partnership between UTSA and the local UT Health Science Center, which conducted research in areas as diverse as biomechanics, cancer biology, computational sciences, and health care disparities.

Another complementary organization was the Texas Biomedical Research Institute, which employed four hundred people. Seventy are doctoral-level scientists who lead about 180 major research projects in areas such as genetics, virology and immunology, physiology and medicine, organic chemistry, and comparative medicine.

Building on the strength of research, SATAI helped more local biotechnology firms attract capital, assisting local medical product firms such as OsteoBiologics, Incell, Vidacare, and Medical Present Value. SATAI also worked with officials at the Texas Research Park to create a biotech incubator and invest in startup technology companies.

In 2005 former mayor Henry Cisneros created the Healthcare Bioscience Development Corporation, which does business as BioMed SA, with Ann Stevens as the first president. Cisneros announced, "We will promote San Antonio to the rest of the world as the best place for bioscience high-tech companies to locate."

A 2004 economic impact study of the city's health care and biomedical industry found it to be more than twice the size it was a decade ago and four times its size in 1993. Its economic impact is some $30 billion. The industry employs some 164,000 workers, many of them in tech-related jobs.

During the 2005 legislative session, SATAI successfully lobbied to create a $200 million Texas Emerging Technology Fund (TETF), to be used for collaborations, investments, research grants, and talent recruitment. Seven Regional Centers of Innovation and Commercialization were created, including one in Bexar County. The governor was authorized to appoint a seventeen-member commission.

On June 29, 2005, I introduced Spencer to Governor Rick Perry, urging his appointment to the commission. Perry said to Spencer, "Get your application in." On August 19 Spencer was named chairman of the commission. SATAI became the San Antonio regional center, with all local recommendations for state funding channeled through it.

A few months later, on the advice of SATAI, two San Antonio

tech firms received grants. CardioSpectra received $1.35 million, and Xilas Medical received $1 million. CardioSpectra sold two years later for $64 million. Investors, including the TETF, received six times their investment. But the investment in Xilas was a failure. The investments illustrated two things about the use of public funds: both its promise and its risk. The volatility of investing in tech companies would prove to be problematic over time.

TETF also made a $3.5 million grant to UTSA and a $6 million grant to the Health Science Center here.

SATAI began to lose its punch over the years. It held on until 2010, when it morphed into the StarTech Foundation, then finally closed its doors in 2013.

Some people will say SATAI did not live up to its promise to grow and diversify the technology industry. Perhaps it was ahead of the curve and thus not able to move the needle as far as some people wanted. But unlike in the Datapoint days, SATAI proved that success can be achieved when federal, state, and local government and nonprofit organizations assist in the diversification of the technology industry. The collaboration helped make significant progress in the biosciences, aerospace, and cybersecurity.

## GRAHAM WESTON AND RACKSPACE

Along with the evolution of the military's role in cybersecurity, biomedicine, and aerospace and SATAI's role in fostering a private sector tech industry, one small tech startup would prove to have a major impact on San Antonio. In 1998 entrepreneur Graham Weston and his sometime partner, Morris Miller, met with three recent Trinity University students, Richard Yoo, Dirk Elmendorf, and Patrick Condon, who were bidding to wire Weston's downtown office tower, the Weston Centre, for internet service. Weston was fascinated by digital technology, and asked the trio a question that he often posed to people who interested him: "If you had all sorts of capital that you could put to good use, what business would you launch?"

The younger men looked knowingly at one another. One asked whether Weston would be willing to sign a nondisclosure agreement, and he agreed. Then they described a business that would allow companies to rent access to computer servers, without having to buy a lot of expensive hardware and operating software. Weston immediately saw the appeal of the idea and agreed to put up the capital. The five founded Rackspace Hosting, and Weston soon became its CEO.

Weston had grown up in the San Antonio area, graduated from Texas A&M University, and gone into the real estate business. He had bought a prominent downtown skyscraper, now known as Weston Centre, for dimes on the dollar in the wake of the 1980s savings and loan crisis. He had a canny sense of timing, both in his real estate investments and with Rackspace.

Rackspace grew to twelve employees its first year and reached $100,000 in sales. The next year, in the face of rising competition, the company decided to differentiate itself around a brand of always-available, can-do customer service that it called "fanatical support." It quickly saw that such support could only be volunteered by employees who took pride in their work and were empowered to spend time and money on customer care.

The company continued to build sales and by 2005 had grown to 1,200 employees with sales of $200 million. That was the year I ran into Weston under unusual circumstances. Our meeting was prompted by a hurricane. On August 29 Hurricane Katrina smashed into the coasts of Mississippi and Louisiana, breaching the levees of New Orleans and causing flooding and devastation. Hurricane Rita followed a few weeks later. Houston was quickly overwhelmed with refugees, and soon thousands of them were streaming into San Antonio.

Mayor Hardberger and I drew up a plan to house them in two vacant buildings on the former Kelly Air Force Base. We soon ran out of room. Then Weston arranged for us to use an abandoned Montgomery Ward store at the shuttered Windsor Park Mall. On Sunday morning after the second hurricane, my son Kevin, then a member of the city council, and I were checking on refugees in the Ward building when we saw Weston talking to some of them. "I'm surprised to see you here helping everyone," I told him. "I don't know of many CEOs that would do this."

"Whenever we do something at Rackspace, we go all in," he said.

As we walked around making sure everyone was all right, Weston told me, "We're running out of room in the old Datapoint production facility. This mall could work for us. I've been talking to Windcrest Mayor Jack Leonhardt." I replied that I had also been talking to Leonhardt about the idea.

The deal would be complicated. It would require special state legislation and then the city would have to transfer the mall into the city limits of Windcrest. In turn, Windcrest, through its economic development agency, would have to buy the 1.2-million-square-foot mall, take it off the tax rolls, and lease it to Rackspace. The county would give a tax abatement on the personal property.

We worked together and finally pulled it off. In 2006 Windcrest Economic Development Corporation entered into a thirty-year lease with Rackspace. We also successfully lobbied the state to make a grant of $22 million to Rackspace, with the provision that it would create four thousand jobs in Texas within five years. Two years later Weston moved the headquarters into the mall. The same year Rackspace went public, raising $187.5 million in capital. Weston was ready to expand, and he did.

In 2009 he selected Lew Moorman, then the company's Chief Strategy Officer, to become president of Rackspace. The scion of two pioneering Texas families, Moorman was a graduate of Duke University and Stanford Law School. He led Rackspace's development of the OpenStack cloud operating system in partnership with NASA. Seven years later Rackspace's annual revenue surpassed $2 billion, and it employed more than six thousand engineers, executives, and other employees worldwide.

In 2010 Weston stepped into a public leadership position in San Antonio when Mayor Julián Castro asked him to join two others in chairing a communitywide visioning effort. SA2020 would set goals to be accomplished by the end of decade.

I had chaired Target 90, a similar effort, some twenty-seven years before, created by Henry Cisneros when he was mayor. We had set goals to be accomplished by 1990 and were successful with 90 percent of them.

I spoke at the SA2020 kick-off meeting of some six hundred people. Weston then spoke of the need to think about big, transformational ideas. One possible goal he mentioned was to create a vibrant urban core in San Antonio—with attractive housing and entertainment venues, and transit options such as ridesharing or streetcars—that would appeal to a young, talented workforce.

The SA2020 report, released one year later, included the goal that was right up Weston's alley: a vibrant, urban, intercity initiative. With the vision in hand, Castro announced that this would be the "Decade of Downtown." He established a "housing-first policy" for downtown and created an incentive fund to encourage housing. This was a brilliant strategy because retail and restaurants follow rooftops, and more office space was likely with a downtown workforce.

This policy also was right in line with the work that the Commissioners Court had begun in the central city. We had invested $108 million in the Tobin Center for the Performing Arts and another $10 million in the Briscoe Western Art Museum and the Alameda Theater. We had invested more than $200 million in the San Antonio River, including environmental restoration of the southern Mission Reach and the northern Museum Reach as far as the Pearl Brewery redevelopment project. We also were in the early planning stages for a $175 million restoration of San Pedro Creek on the near West Side.

The Commissioners Court also extended our Tax Abatement Program to include downtown multifamily units. The program proved successful, and multifamily developments started popping up all over the central city.

In the same year that the SA2020 report came out, Weston founded the 80/20 Foundation and appointed Lorenzo Gomez president. Based on the Pareto principle, the foundation would invest in the 20 percent of nonprofits that drive 80 percent of the impact to turn San Antonio into a hub for entrepreneurship, promote technology education for high-skilled jobs, and provide more options for people to live, work, and play in the urban core of San Antonio.

At the same time, Weston, with fellow tech entrepreneur Nick Longo, founded a coworking space called Geekdom. The purpose was to bring tech startups together in a single location that provided dirt-cheap rent along with support for their companies. In exchange, the startups had to agree to spend at least one hour a week sharing their skills with other Geekdom members. Weston provided the space without the usual requirement of an equity position in the startup companies.

He said Geekdom's success would be judged by how many startup companies succeeded in its first ten years. Geekdom was originally located in the Weston Center, but Weston bought the downtown Rand Building and converted the whole building into space for startups. While he moved forward with Geekdom and the 80/20 Foundation, Mayor Castro wasted no time in moving the tech industry forward in renewable energy. In the 1990s I served on the CPS Energy board for some nine years when we took the first steps into renewable energy by contracting for wind energy. Now CPS Energy draws from a large network of wind turbines.

Castro expanded the scope of renewable energy when he teamed up with CPS Energy CEO Doyle Beneby to create a large footprint for solar power. They announced that CPS Energy would build a 400-megawatt solar farm. They entered into an economic development agreement with Korea-based Nexelon, an affiliate of OCI, to build a $130 million, 240,000-square-foot Mission Solar Energy plant at Brooks City-Base, which opened in 2015.

Six solar companies, taking advantage of a $30 million CPS Energy rebate program for rooftop solar, located their offices at Geekdom.

Weston took another big step in 2012 when he founded Weston Urban. Randy Smith, a lawyer and the former vice president of real estate for Rackspace, became its president. Weston Urban's goal was to create a unique urban environment in San Antonio where people could live, work, walk, shop, dine, hear live music, and enjoy urban parks. It would work with the 80/20 Foundation and Geekdom to accomplish its goal.

I began meeting with Smith as he targeted the near West Side as an opportunity for redevelopment. He was interested in the restoration of San Pedro Creek. I assured him the county was moving ahead on the project, working to have the first phase completed by May 2018, the three hundredth anniversary of San Antonio's founding.

To kick things off, Smith and Weston struck a major development agreement with Frost Bank and the city of San Antonio. In June 2014 they joined then-Mayor Castro and City Manager Sheryl Sculley to announce that Weston Urban would build a twenty-three-floor glass skyscraper with Class A office space and a parking garage to be occupied by Frost Bank and other tenants. The building, the first downtown high-rise to be built in more than a quarter-century, would be located on the site of the Frost Motor Bank adjacent to San Pedro Creek, facing Houston Street.

Under the agreement, Weston Urban acquired the old twenty-two-story Frost Bank Tower and parking garage and traded it to the city, which would use it for office space, consolidating agencies that were scattered across several smaller buildings. In exchange, the city would give Weston Urban the Municipal Plaza Building (the city council chamber will remain there on the first floor), the old Continental Hotel (occupied by Metro Health), the former San Fernando Gym, and a strip of property on Main Avenue. On the properties that Weston Urban acquired from the city, it would build some three hundred residential units.

As part of the deal, the county agreed to a $3 million grant, funded through the Houston Street TIRZ, for the new Frost Bank tower. This was a game-changing deal that complemented the investment the county was making along San Pedro Creek.

Weston Urban would go on to buy the Milam Building on Travis Street and the Savoy Building on Houston Street across from the Rand Building, where Geekdom is located.

At the same time, Kevin Covey, who founded GrayStreet Partners and is its managing partner, began accumulating property on the east end of Houston Street. A six-block spine of Houston Street would connect Weston Urban properties to Covey's. He also purchased the Vogue Building and located web developer Turner Logic and SpaceCadet in the building, as well as Michael Girdley's Codeup, which offered software-training classes. In 2016 he recruited Easy Expunctions from Austin to locate there.

GrayStreet also acquired the vacant Kress Building on Houston Street with plans to create 80,000 square feet of office space and a 15,000-square-foot food hall, modeled on Mercado Roma in Mexico City. In late 2016 we provided financial incentives to Capture RX, a medical tech firm. CEO and founder Chris Hotchkiss will expand his 114 employees to 400 and locate in the Kress Building once the improvements are finished.

In 2016 Covey bought Travis Park Plaza, a few blocks from Weston Urban's Milam Building, and began remodeling it to accommodate tech firms, installing high-speed fiber-optic internet, common lounges, and recreational areas.

As Weston Urban and GrayStreet Partners moved ahead with their respective ends of the downtown technology district, H-E-B announced in October 2013 that it would expand its corporate offices on the near south end of downtown, two blocks from the county courthouse. Over a period of years, the company would add one thousand employees to its campus, many in tech-related jobs. The expansion would require closing a portion of Main Street, which the Commissioners Court supported and the city council approved. H-E-B also announced that it would build the city's first downtown grocery store. The 12,000-square-foot store, located next to its campus, opened in December 2015.

The near east end of downtown also saw a lot of action. The city created the Hemisfair Park Area Redevelopment Corporation to assist in the redevelopment of Hemisfair Park, site of the 1968 World's Fair. In spring 2011 it held public hearings and developed a mixed-use master plan, which the city council approved in spring 2012.

As part of the plan, the convention center would be expanded and a portion of the original center would be demolished to provide more park space, as well as housing, retail, and a small hotel. The federal courthouse on the grounds would be repositioned or demolished. Plans already were under way for a new federal courthouse to be built one block west of the Bexar County Courthouse. Federal funding has been secured, and the construction company has been selected.

United Services Automobile Association (USAA), founded in San Antonio in 1924, became a major player in reviving the downtown. Since 1924 it has evolved into a company that offers banking, insurance, financial planning, and investment services. Today it is a $27 billion company with nearly thirty-three thousand employees, nineteen thousand of whom work in San Antonio.

After Stuart Parker became CEO-elect in 2014, I hosted him and his leadership team at the courthouse for a half-day-long meeting. We talked about various issues facing our city and the major projects that the city and county were working on. We spent time talking about the evolving tech industry and downtown development.

USAA had purchased the One Riverwalk building, located downtown at 700 North St. Marys Street, in 2013. Senior Vice President Harriet Dominique was assigned to be the site leader. Some four hundred USAA employees were transferred to the new building, including some one hundred members of the company's innovation team, giving a big boost to the tech district.

In August 2017 USAA purchased the Bank of America Plaza. On December 14, 2017, the company announced that it would assign two thousand employees to the downtown building and add 1,500 new jobs across San Antonio.

During the same time frame that USAA was making these decisions, its executive vice president, Wayne Peacock, became chairman of the Economic Development Foundation, a city-county and private sector organization to foster job creation. Under his leadership the foundation expanded its mission to include job training and concentrated on attracting higher-paying jobs.

In 2016 CPS Energy, under the leadership of CEO Paula Gold-Williams and Board Chair Ed Kelley, purchased the long-abandoned AT&T building, located downtown on the River Walk. The building would be renovated and serve as their headquarters.

The Decade of Downtown announced by Castro is off and running. From San Pedro Creek on the west to Hemisfair Park on the east, transformation is under way. From the Pearl District north of downtown to rapid development around Southtown, the city's center core is strengthening. A vibrant urban area, long overdue, is already attracting a young, talented workforce that will help expand the downtown tech district. I believe Weston likes that.

## TECH BLOC

Controversy ignites flames of passion and many times paves the way for something new and positive. In December 2014 the city drew up an unreasonably restrictive ordinance to regulate transportation network companies—Uber and Lyft—that had been operating in San Antonio during the previous year. This flickering flame soon lit a fire under a new generation of techies.

On December 9 Weston wrote a letter to Mayor Ivy Taylor and the city council urging them to postpone a vote on the ordinance. He said the ordinance would undermine progress to promote San Antonio as a city on the rise, not a city that restricts new technologies through regulation. He also said Rackspace must attract and retain young talent, many of whom want an urban life with modern transportation options.

I followed up with a letter the next day to Taylor and the council urging postponement and supporting Uber and Lyft. Unfortunately Taylor led the effort to pass the restrictive ordinance on a 7–2 vote, with two abstentions. Both companies said they would leave when the ordinance took effect, and they made good on that threat.

In addition to meeting with the San Antonio mayor biweekly, I also meet with the mayors of the other twenty-six cities in Bexar County. They shared my view that the transportation services were important. On March 6, 2015, I wrote a letter asking the companies to continue serving the other twenty-six cities and the unincorporated areas of Bexar County. Uber accepted, and service continued.

The controversy galvanized the tech community to become politically active. Former Rackspace president Lew Moorman led the effort to create a tech advocacy organization, which he named Tech Bloc. David Heard of SecureLogix, Tom Cuthbert of Vistage/Adometry, David Spencer of Prytime (previously Pryor Medical Devices), Lorenzo Gomez of 80/20 Foundation, and Brad Parscale of Giles-Parscale joined the effort. Marina Alderete Gavito, formerly a Rackspace senior product manager, was hired as executive director.

After the creation of Tech Bloc was announced, Weston called and asked me to support Moorman. "Lew is smart and a strategic thinker," he said. "He knows what he is doing." I signed on.

On May 19 Mayor Taylor and I attended Tech Bloc's kickoff event, where more than nine hundred tech industry leaders gathered at Southerleigh Fine Food and Brewery at the Pearl. Moorman's pumped-up speech emphasized the importance of Uber and Lyft and urged the city to work out a reasonable ordinance. He said Tech Bloc also wanted to improve technology education, create an urban lifestyle, develop public policies to strengthen the city's emerging technology sector, and help build a growing modern economy.

Tech Bloc's kickoff could not have come at a better time. Just three days later I was scheduled to give my annual North San Antonio Chamber of Commerce speech, which focused on the tech industry. Over several months I had met with tech leaders to get their input. Here is an edited selection from the speech I gave to the North San Antonio Chamber of Commerce on May 22:

All elements of our economy are affected by the rapid innovation technology brings. The explosive growth of computing power, storage, networking, and software applications is rapidly changing the economy. The dynamics of the job market are changing before our eyes.

Successful twenty-first-century cities will be judged by their willingness and ability to enter into this new economy that is defined by these innovative and often disruptive technologies. But we are slipping behind other cities in our efforts to embrace this new emerging tech industry. We need to pick up our pace, or we will be eclipsed.

There is hope and a new rumbling in town. On Tuesday I attended Lew Moorman's Tech Bloc kickoff event with over nine hundred tech industry leaders. Lew Moorman's speech at Tech Bloc's rally emphasized the importance of Uber and Lyft, improving livability, new economic development policies, and marketing of the city's strength in emerging technology.

There was electricity in the room and an excitement I have not seen before. New leadership is stepping up to push our city forward. If we will step up and support them, we could become a thriving innovative tech city.

The county did that with BiblioTech when we opened the nation's first all-digital public library in 2013. It was a challenge to the old way of doing business. We are bringing technology and ebooks and adding more tech courses.

I also announced the county would create a $1 million innovation fund to grow small tech companies and support skilled training in high schools. It would be administered by our economic development department, created in 2005 and directed by David Marquez. Marquez, who has a master's degree in urban administration from Trinity University and teaches part time at the University of the Incarnate Word, had come to work for the county in 1997 and had managed the construction and ongoing operations of the AT&T Center, Bexar County's arena.

I also committed county financial support for the recently created Chamber of Commerce cybersecurity industry task force, chaired by John Dickson and administered by Will Garrett, who has a master's in business administration from UTSA. I supported restructuring the Economic Development Foundation to focus on talent development and the emerging technology sector.

The speech and the Tech Bloc rally may have had some impact on the city council. Taylor asked City Manager Sculley to draft a less restrictive ordinance regulating the ride-sharing business. Councilman Roberto Treviño chaired the council committee that steered the city toward a workable ordinance.

In August 2015 an ordinance was passed on a 6–5 vote: Taylor and Councilman Joe Krier had voted no on the previous ordinance, but now voted yes. While it was disappointing that the vote was so close, it did pass. The taxi industry had a strong hold on several council members, and they did not relent. Tech Bloc had won its first political victory, and another soon followed.

For the previous two years city leaders had tried to persuade Google Fiber to come to San Antonio. Its internet speed of eleven megabytes per second was about a hundred times faster than the basic broadband connections.

Mark Strama, head of Google Fiber in Texas, is a former state representative whom I supported when he first ran for the Texas legislature. I spoke to him a few times, encouraging Google to come to San Antonio.

In August 2015 Google finally announced it would come here

but, as this book goes to press, they have stumbled on implementing a plan to lay four thousand linear miles of fiber-optic line and are looking at other ways to expand their system. Meanwhile, their announcement caused AT&T to upgrade their internet speed. Google also partnered with BiblioTech to provide computers and technical assistance to public housing residents, enabling them to have internet connections in their apartments, many for the first time. The county provided one hundred computers, and Google funded personnel costs.

The year 2015 continued to be big for tech. In addition to Google Fiber and the council approval of transportation network companies, Weston and UTSA stepped up in a big way to create the Open Cloud Institute. At the February 26 announcement ceremony, UTSA President Ricardo Romo said the university would develop degree programs in cloud computing and big data in a partnership with the tech industry to position the city as a world leader in open cloud technology.

Weston said the program would accelerate the industry with an explosion of innovation in scientific research. His 80/20 Foundation contributed $4.8 million to the program. UTSA is now one of the leaders of academia in cloud, cybersecurity, computing, and analytics.

Tech initiatives did not slow in 2016. In March I began meeting with Kate Rogers, vice president of communications and health promotion at H-E-B, about the possibility of a downtown high school. Rogers said it would operate as a charter school in the San Antonio School District, and H-E-B Chairman Charles Butt would make a significant donation.

At Tech Bloc's first birthday party on June 16, Rogers

announced the new tech high school. She said that Butt would give $3.7 million to the school. I said BiblioTech would provide services and books to the school library.

A few days later, on June 23, tech leaders announced creation of a cybersecurity incubator at Geekdom called Build Sec Foundry. The goal was to provide tactical and financial support for startups, helping them to grow into larger firms. The hope was that many of them would join some thirty local private cybersecurity head-quarters and sixty key offices for cybersecurity.

Bexar County economic deputy director Jordana Decamps, who earned a degree in political science and Spanish from SMU, was instrumental in administering the innovation funds. She allocated funds to assist small firms and those taking tech courses at Codeup and Open Cloud Academy. She funded $50,000 for a Tech Fuel competition administered by Tech Bloc. The winners were SnackDot, Rising Barn, and MilTribe, in that order. Veterans were provided scholarships for Open Cloud Academy. The Fund also supported CompTIA training at BiblioTech, offset certificate testing costs at local high schools, and provided apprenticeship opportunities with Codeup. The fund was also used to attract three new technology companies to downtown San Antonio: Easy Expunctions (Austin), Dialpad (San Francisco), and Liquid Web (Lansing).

The community stepped up to support the Air Force Association's CyberPatriot program, which inspires students toward careers in cybersecurity through a National Youth Cyber Defense Competition. The Cyber Texas Foundation, led by Joe Sanchez Jr. and Chris Cook, hosted the San Antonio event. In 2015 local and regional schools fielded 198 teams, more than any other city. Two of those teams advanced to the national championship.

San Antonio remains on a technology roll. Shaun Williams, who chairs an IT industry council called SA-Tecosystem, released a study showing that local tech jobs grew from fifteen thousand in 2008 to thirty-four thousand in 2016. The total economic impact is $10 billion. The average wage is $78,000 a year, compared to $45,000 across the overall San Antonio economy.

Rackspace is still the leading local tech company, with a market capitalization of $3.68 billion. Of its 6,100 employees worldwide, about 3,300 work in San Antonio. Since 2007 it has appeared on the Fortune 100 "best companies to work for" list six of seven years.

For all its success, Rackspace has seen plenty of setbacks and disruptions. It struggled for several years competing head-to-head against the big cloud infrastructure providers Amazon Web Services, Google, and Microsoft. Rackspace's revenue growth slowed, and its stock price declined. In early 2014 the company began to receive inquiries from companies interested in acquiring it or partnering with it. Rackspace hired Morgan Stanley to explore its options, later deciding to remain independent.

In 2015, under new CEO Taylor Rhodes, Rackspace shifted away from competition with the industry giants and instead formed partnerships with them. It began providing expertise and support for business customers who wanted to use Amazon Web Services, Microsoft Azure, and other third-party cloud platforms. These lines of business grew rapidly, but rumors continued that Rackspace would either be taken over by a larger company or go private.

On August 4, 2016, the *Wall Street Journal* reported that Rackspace was in talks with private equity firms. Speculation ran high about who might buy the company and at what price. Its stock price increased 10 percent. Weston and I traded text messages on August 5. I texted: "I know you are covered up. Let me know what to do at the right time." His response: "I hope you understand that I can't comment on what's in the press right now." I replied that I did.

The next day it was reported that Apollo Global Management was in talks with Rackspace. Founded in 1990 and based in New York City, Apollo managed more than $173 billion in assets. I had some knowledge of the firm. In 1999 our family had sold Sun Harvest, our natural food business, to Wild Oats Marketplace, a national natural food chain. Whole Foods Market eventually bought Wild Oats and sold the Sun Harvest division to Apollo. I tried to buy the business back from Apollo, but we failed to reach an agreement. Apollo later sold Sun Harvest to Sprouts Farmers Market, a national chain of natural food supermarkets.

On August 26 Rackspace and Apollo announced a definitive agreement for certain funds managed by affiliates of Apollo to purchase Rackspace, which would then operate as a private company. The deal would be subject to a vote of shareholders, who seemed likely to approve since they would receive a 34 percent premium to the stock price before the reports of a sale were published. The national headquarters for Rackspace would remain in San Antonio with the same leadership team. Apollo made clear that it was buying a company that was growing and profitable and that it planned to help Rackspace structure itself for more rapid growth over a period of years.

Rackspace's evolution was similar to Datapoint's. Both companies had a great run for years, strong competition evolved, sales growth stalled, stocks went down, and, eventually, both went private. But there is major difference: Rackspace, unlike Datapoint, is profitable and still growing sales. So there is hope.

At lunch the day before the announced sale, Moorman, who still serves on the Rackspace board, and I caught up on several issues. He told me about a venture he had launched called Scaleworks. "We buy small software companies that we feel we can accelerate and relocate them to San Antonio," he said. "We already have four here." I told him that was great news and asked what would happen with Rackspace.

"Rackspace will be around for a long time," he said.

We talked about Tech Bloc, a proposed new baseball stadium, commuter rail service to Austin and his extraordinary family. (Wildcatter Tom Slick was his paternal great-grandfather. Tom Slick Jr., founder of Southwest Research Institute and Southwest Biomedical Research Institute, was his great uncle. Former Federal District Judge John Wood Jr., who was assassinated here in 1979, was his maternal grandfather.)

After the lunch I felt much better about Rackspace—and even better after Weston and I discussed Apollo's plans. He explained that Apollo saw Rackspace as a growth investment. He said he would have more time and capital to invest in downtown development. According to SEC filings, he would receive more than $600 million for his stock.

I met with David Sambur, an Apollo senior partner, in New York on November 22. During our half-hour visit, we talked about my family's grocery business that they had purchased, Trump's election, Sambur's proposed quarterly visits to San Antonio, and Weston and Rackspace. He said Apollo was happy with San Antonio and had confidence in Rackspace's leadership. He said he believed that Rackspace would grow in volume and profits but would first have to adjust the workforce and cut some expenses.

I was confident that the Apollo deal would benefit Rackspace, its shareholders (many of whom, like Weston, work and invest in San Antonio), and the city.

Rackspace's new CEO, Joe Eazor, helped us attract another tech-related firm. In early March 2017 I met Hulu's senior vice president, Ben Smith, at Rackspace. Hulu, an on-demand internet streaming media, is a joint venture with the Walt Disney Company, 21st Century Fox, Comcast, and Time Warner. It had narrowed a search for a new viewer experience headquarters from twenty-three cities to three, and we were one of the finalists. He was impressed with Rackspace's operation and San Antonio's workforce.

On March 7, at the crack of dawn, Mayor Ivy Taylor, Jordana Decamps, who by now had been promoted to Bexar County economic director, an EDF delegation led by President Jenna Saucedo-Herrera, and I took off for Los Angeles airport to meet with Hulu's CEO, CFO, and SVPS. We made our closing argument for why San Antonio was the best site for Hulu to establish their viewer experience headquarters, then headed back to the airport. We got to San Antonio at midnight.

That sealed the deal. They chose us and decided on a building right off IH-10 near the medical district. Hulu will add a dimension to our evolving tech industry, creating five hundred jobs.

According to Tech Bloc, San Antonio now has some one thousand tech companies, of which nine hundred are small firms. As we worked to create additional tech education programs, we were still not meeting the industry's demands for a talented workforce. Because the vast number of San Antonio's tech companies are small, Tech Bloc wanted to create a "chief talent and recruitment officer" to assist small firms in finding talent, either homegrown or recruited to our city. A database would track available jobs and worker seeking employment, and a website would showcase our emerging central city tech industry. We agreed to support the program. In July 2017 the Commissioners Court approved $180,000 to support the tech office and the website.

That month the Commissioners Court took another step to broaden the scope of technology. We began work on an idea that Ken Villano, Bexar County chief innovation officer, brought forward in 2016. Villano, who had worked for five years at Rackspace, proposed establishing kiosks in the central city that would provide free Wi-Fi and a touch screen with access to a city map, directions, information, and governmental services. He contacted CIVIQ, a startup company in New York that was in the process of installing one thousand kiosks around New York City.

County Manager David Smith and I went to New York, met with CIVIQ officials, and toured several of the kiosks. We asked the company to design one for San Antonio that would withstand the Texas heat. After several months of negotiations led by Assistant County Manager Thomas Guevara, we reached an agreement. The kiosk they designed was significantly better than the ones in New York. Monica Ramos, a public information officer with a master's degree in political science from St. Mary's University, was charged with rolling out the initiative.

On July 20, 2017, Ramos held a press conference in the county purchasing department's warehouse to reveal the nine-foot-high kiosk, which had large touch screens on both sides. Phillip Rico, the information technology network architect who had designed the software, gave a demonstration.

Mohammad Benhalim, project director for Bexar County

Facilities, announced that we would install six kiosks in the downtown area. Forty-five days later, on September 1, we had them operational. I said that this was another step in moving San Antonio forward as a "smart city" and that we would seek to expand the number of kiosks by partnering with private sector participants, the city, and our public transportation authority, VIA.

A few days later Taylor Eighmy was selected as the next president of UTSA. Within a few months he began developing plans to enlarge the UTSA downtown campus, and in summer 2018 he revealed his plan to Mayor Ron Nirenberg and me. It included a School of Data Science, a National Security Collaboration Center, and a new College of Business. Nirenberg and I committed to make seven acres of county and city land available alongside San Pedro Creek extending from Nueva Street to Dolorosa Street. UT Board of Regents member Brad Weaver committed the university to $70 million in funding, and Graham Weston donated $15 million. The business school would be financed by tuition-backed bonds.

On September 18 we held a press conference announcing the most important strategic investment ever made in downtown, one that would complement our emerging tech district and help catalyze future downtown development.

I stepped back into the past glory days of Datapoint when I paid a visit to the office of David Monroe, president of e-Watch Corporation, a local software developer for surveillance camera systems. He had worked at Datapoint with the team led by Poor that invented the first microprocessor, which made personal computers possible. Monroe had invited me to see a huge collection of Datapoint artifacts. He hopes to create a technology museum one day.

He showed me the Datapoint 2200 computer, random-access

memory products, and the first solid-state memory product. I saw a 1970 Computer Terminal Corporation purchase order to Intel for $3 million worth of semiconductor processors. The order said the processors were developed by Intel and Computer Terminal and there would be no charge unless Intel met the specifications of their joint agreement. Intel went on to become a successful company because of the eight-bit processor that Poor and his team had led in developing. Datapoint, successor to Computer Terminal, lost all rights to the processor.

I marveled at how far ahead of everyone else this city had been back in the 1970s and early 1980s. We had it all and lost it. But I found comfort in the fact that, in the unlikely event that Rackspace were to falter as Datapoint did, San Antonio would be judged smarter this time. The tech industry is more diversified. Rackspace helped make that happen when it encouraged former Rackers to contribute to companies such as Scaleworks, Assembla, Chargify, Codeup, Jungledisk, Filestack, Promoter IQ, TrueAbility, HelpSocial, and ScaleFT.

The city has strong footholds in biotechnology, private and military cybersecurity, academia, and embedded technology in large companies such as H-E-B, Valero, USAA, and Tesoro. It has a thriving group of tech entrepreneurs and investors and a great partnership between local government and the tech community.

We are on the right tech track. With our technology diversification, San Antonio is positioned to be a leading innovative city. But technology changes faster than the earth spins, so the city must continue to embrace technology even when it might disrupt existing (and often politically active) industries. It has to continue to support tech startups and remain resilient in the face of the failures that are a necessary element for long-term success in technology.

# SIX

## *BiblioTech*

IN THE SUMMER OF 2012, as I was reading Walter Isaacson's book on Steve Jobs, I became caught up in the strange and exciting life of that quirky nonconformist. Jobs envisioned a new reality and was determined to take all of us there. A marketing genius, a gambler, and a ruthless competitor, he demanded excellence from his team. He understood which products to develop and how consumers would react to them.

After Jobs successfully developed the iMac computer and laptop, he began moving Apple away from an emphasis on computers to mobile electronic devices and applications. The digital mobile revolution took off in 2007 when Jobs released the iPhone. In the same year, Amazon launched the Kindle ereader. The following year, BooksOnBoard became the first to sell ebooks over smartphones, and Barnes & Noble released the Nook. In January 2010 Jobs trotted out the iPad, which had access to the internet. It included the same touch-screen-based operating system as the iPhone and could be an ebook reader.

By the time I read Isaacson's book in 2012, annual sales of ebook titles had grown from 10 million in 2008 to 457 million.

Amazon became a major player in the ebook market by using its market muscle and pricing to control about two-thirds of the ebook market. It sold some ebooks below cost, with selected best-sellers available at $9.99.

The evolution of ebooks reminded me of Robert Carlton Brown's prophecy. In 1930 he wrote, "The written word has not kept up with the age. The movies have outmaneuvered it. We have the talkies, but as yet no readies. Enough with the tyranny of paper and ink! Writing has been bottled up in books since the start. It's time to pull out the stopper and begin a bloody revolution of the word." The revolution that he envisioned started in 1971 when Michael Hart launched Project Gutenberg, a book collection available over the internet. It enabled people to download noncopyrighted books and documents in electronic form onto their desktop computers. This development was considered the birth of ebooks.

Later the Internet Archive and Google would lay the groundwork for a quantum leap in digitizing existing books and information. The Internet Archive began digitizing more than one thousand books a day. In October 2004 Google introduced Google Print at the Frankfurt Book Fair. It used the Elphel 323 camera to scan at a rate of one thousand pages per hour. In 2010 Google announced that it intended to scan all known 129,864,880 books. By 2012 it had scanned some 30 million books.

Unfortunately Jobs did not live long enough to see the explosion of the mobile digital revolution. The year after the iPad came out, on August 24, 2011, Jobs announced his resignation as CEO of Apple through an email. He died six weeks later. He had delayed treatment of a less aggressive form of pancreatic cancer that was considered treatable and curable. Instead he relied on an alternative diet of natural foods and health remedies. Many doctors believe that his delay in seeking traditional medical treatment cost him his life.

When I finished reading Isaacson's book, it hit me that I lived in a world that had rapidly changed since the 2007 iPhone and would continue to change rapidly in the future. The mobile digital revolution had exploded in five short years. It offered an opportunity to break down barriers to access to reading and information. If economically disadvantaged people received free access to ebooks, ebook readers, technology, and training, they could enter the digital world. I was inspired to move forward with an idea of how to do that.

As it happened, at the time I was reading the Jobs book, Bexar County was having a problem with the San Antonio Public Library. The county had been giving the city library system $3.8 million annually to allow residents of unincorporated areas to check out books. Now the city system was demanding $6.6 million. The most any county in Texas contributed to city libraries was $200,000. What were those library leaders thinking?

I had read the 2011 study funded by the San Antonio Public Library reporting that public libraries needed to do more to expose students to digital literacy and media literacy, skills essential for accessing, processing, and communicating information. According to the American Library Association, however, public libraries spent only 12.4 percent on digital materials from their $1.26 billion budgets for library collections. Public libraries continued to rely on printed books, with limited investment in technology. The San Antonio library system was like other public libraries in that regard.

During the 1940s my mother would take my brother and me

to the public library. We boarded a bus at the corner of Presa Street and McKinley Avenue on the near South Side and made our way downtown. San Antonio's grand Art Deco/neoclassical, three-story library building was on the corner of Presa and Market Streets. Built of cut Indiana limestone, the 38,000-square-foot library was the pride of San Antonio. Inscriptions on the east and west sides of the building included a quote by Ralph Waldo Emerson: "Books are the home of the American people."

My parents were working-class folks striving to enter the middle class, and the public library was important to my family. My grandparents on my father's side lived with us. Living and working together, my family stretched its earned dimes to enter the fringes of the middle class.

Printed books were the library's stock-in-trade, and the library's responsibility was to provide those books to their patrons. The librarian indexed them, arranged them by subject matter on shelves, and helped patrons make their selections. The library also provided collections of research materials such as newspapers, local history documents, census results, and government documents. Teen activities, story times, learning activities, and summer reading programs evolved. Libraries stuck to their roots even as the mobile digital revolution rapidly moved ahead. They continued to build expensive branch libraries averaging some fifteen thousand square feet, stuffing them with hard-copy books and ignoring or giving token consideration to ebooks.

A June 2012 Pew Research Center survey of library patrons that found 62 percent did not know whether their library offered ebooks. Lower-income households showed interest in borrowing preloaded ereading devices, taking classes about how to use the devices, and downloading books. With the changing digital world, the Pew Center report defined patrons in a different way. If people had done one of three things in the past twelve months, they were considered library patrons: visited a public library in person; visited a public library website; or used a cell phone, ereader, or tablet to visit a public library website or access public library resources. In two of the three criteria, people did not need to physically go to a public library to be considered patrons.

After digesting this information, I thought it was time for the county to try a new, and possibly groundbreaking, path. I thought we could create a digital library, focusing solely on ebooks and information available over the internet. People throughout Bexar County could check out books without going to an expensive library location. This approach would save money and break down barriers to reading and information.

We could locate small branch libraries in economically disadvantaged areas where patrons needed computers, laptops, ebook readers, and educational games. With great staffing, we could help people enter the digital world. Without physical books, I believed that branch libraries could be built from one-fourth to one-third the size of traditional fifteen-thousand-square-foot branch libraries and operated with considerably smaller staffs.

It might seem strange for a guy who had been devoted to the San Antonio Public Library system and who had never read an ebook to think about creating a virtual central library in the cloud to support as many digital library branches as might be needed. After all, my relationship with the San Antonio Public Library began when I was elected to the city council in 1987. I successfully led an effort to increase the library budget by $1 million, and in my second year on the council, I supported Mayor Henry Cisneros's $46.4 million bond package, which earmarked $28 million for a new central library. The balance of funding was to build eight adult literacy centers and expand or replace seventeen branch libraries.

The bonds passed with 55 percent of the vote. On the same election date, former Mayor Lila Cockrell was elected mayor, and I was reelected to the council.

After the bond issue passed, I chaired a nine-member advisory board to the council that recommended Romana Plaza on the northern edge of downtown to accommodate a central library. The city council concurred. In May 1991, as library plans moved forward, I ran for mayor and won.

A few weeks later, Ricardo Legorreta, a noted Mexican architect, was chosen as the principal architect. Legorreta designed a building of triangles, rectangles, spheres, squares, arrow windows, and a six-story atrium. Clever use of natural light made the library a mysterious and people-friendly space in which to read and contemplate. The first and second floors had courtyards. Legorreta used bold colors of purple, yellow, and reddish pink, inside and outside.

My wife, Tracy, along with Maria Cossio, executive director of the San Antonio Library Foundation, led an effort to raise $5 million for the central library. I agreed to match the funds with another $5 million from the city.

On the night of May 20, 1995, Tracy and I hosted a grand party in our new 240,000-square-foot central library. More than one thousand people attended the evening gala at two hundred dollars a person to benefit the library foundation. Guests had a great time exploring the building's six floors. We danced into the late evening hours on the second-story patio.

Great cities across the nation built central libraries that were monuments to civic pride and iconic symbols of learning. These libraries defined the city's commitment to accumulating and dispensing knowledge. With its new central library, San Antonio stamped a visible impression on its commitment to learning.

Legorreta went on to win the prestigious Gold Medal, the highest award from the American Institute of Architects. He joined the company of Frank Lloyd Wright, Frank Gehry, and other distinguished architects. Tracy and I remained friends with Legorreta until he died at age eighty in December 2011.

When we opened the library in 1995, no one questioned the role of a large central library. Physical books and documents still dominated the scene. But troublesome signs were emerging. The virtual world of the internet was expanding. In 1991 the first website was created, and the first search protocol (Gopher) that examined files rather than file names was launched. The graphical web browser Mosaic was launched in 1992. The following year Netscape Navigator made the internet easily accessible for non-techies. Two years later, in 1995, commercialization of the internet took hold when Netscape developed an encryption system that made it safer to conduct financial transactions. The year the library opened, Microsoft released Windows 95, an operating system that included a graphical interface and the mouse. It became the dominant operating system.

But ebooks and ebook readers were still in the distance. The only threat to physical books had come in 1993, when Digital Books Incorporated produced the first fifty books in a digital format on floppy disk—not much of a challenge. No one foresaw how quickly technological advancement and the internet would creep up on public libraries. When we opened the central library in 1995, the beginning of the mobile digital revolution was only twelve years away. That was the point at which the ebook revolution and the internet would threaten the traditional role of public libraries.

Over the years, I had become a pretty serious bibliophile, growing to love the beauty of collectable books. I visited used and antiquarian bookstores around the nation and collected modern first editions. I liked the unique settings of small used bookstores, where I could hang out and talk with the owner. I liked to walk the dark, cluttered, narrow walkways between rows of books, finally stumbling across a book that I never would have thought of buying until I grasped it in my hand. Great treasures were hidden away, and when I found one, it was a joy.

The some two thousand books in my library gave me a secure, serene feeling. I appreciated their physicality, sizes, weights, bindings, and paper. I liked to feel the quality and type of paper and to compare the fonts book designers use. The artwork of the book cover brings the artist and the author together, creating so much more than a painting hanging on the wall. Many of my dust jackets are beautiful pieces of artwork. Together on my bookshelf, the books combine to create a different work of art. The colorful spines, sizes, and mixed colors change each time I add a book.

In summer 2012 I wanted to be part of the beckoning new world, but I was pained at the thought of turning my back on my beautiful books and the traditional library. I found a compromise. I would start reading ebooks but also buy the hard copies for my library. The county would continue to support the San Antonio library, but not at the price it demanded.

Once a week I had breakfast at Tommy's Restaurant across the street from the courthouse. A few colleagues usually joined me: David Smith, county manager; David Marquez, economic development director; Laura Jesse, public information officer; and Thomas Guevara, chief of staff to the county manager. Sometimes one of the county commissioners or other members of the county management team also dropped by.

These informal breakfasts provided an opportunity to enjoy each other's company and to bat around ideas. As I read the Jobs book, I shared with them some of the great stories of Apple's innovations and how quickly they came about. We talked about the fast-paced digital revolution, the expansion of ebooks and new reading platforms, and the lack of adequate response by public libraries. I also gave them copies of the Pew report and the San Antonio Public Library's study.

I suggested that the county form a task force that would meet weekly to plan the development of a digital library modeled on the format of a retail store. Because we would be selling a new concept to library patrons, I thought we would have to create a unique store that offered the best products and service. I knew a little about how to do that. I had extensive experience in opening and operating retail stores on the cutting edge of new industries.

In the 1960s my dad and my two brothers and I started a building material business. We were the first local company to build large showrooms and cater to the retail trade. We expanded to nine locations throughout South Texas and sold the business in 1977.

In 1979 my two brothers and I, along with our friends Ron and Don Herrmann, opened the first natural food supermarket, Sun Harvest Farms, in San Antonio. We opened our sixteen-thousand-square-foot store before Whole Foods Market opened its first store in Austin. Never before had San Antonio consumers been offered fresh organic and natural produce, meats, and thousands of other natural and organic food products and vitamins. We were on the cutting edge of a new industry that would become a health mantra to millions of people. We eventually built more stores in San Antonio, Austin, McAllen, El Paso, and Corpus Christi. In 1999 we sold them to a national chain.

As CEO of Sun Harvest, I had developed six principles to guide our operation and expansion. Although our digital library would offer different products and services, the principles were the same. We had to be creative, competitive, and unique, and we had to understand our customers just as in my retail business.

1. *Our mission must be clear, concise, and limited.* We would provide digital books and information through the virtual world. We would create retail-like physical locations in economically disadvantaged areas of the city. With community partners we would create various education programs for our patrons. As we grew, we would not need a physical central library, as our library books would be in the cloud.

2. *We would provide our customers with the best quality products.* We would buy the best computers, laptops, tablets, ereaders, and interactive learning games for children. We would have an annual budget that supported continuously adding titles to a quality collection of ebooks.

3. *We would provide the best customer service.* Our library needed a team with people skills and technology skills. We needed a first-class librarian who believed in the virtual world of books and information.

4. *We would create a unique and exciting store.* We needed a forward look that exemplified the new technology world. It

needed to be a fun, working, collaborative space, different than any existing library.

5. *We would promote our products and services.* While many public libraries offered ebooks and technology, they did not promote them. We would work hard to promote our products and services.

6. *We would act as if a competitor were on our heels.* Because government is noncompetitive, it faces no incentive to move fast, think too far into the future, or take risks. We needed to act as if we were in the private sector. We needed to be cost-effective and willing to make adjustments based on our customers' needs. We needed to stay up-to-date with changing technological advances and to develop different platforms to expand our collection of ebooks.

I shared the principles with my county teammates as the idea of a digital library began to catch everybody's imagination. We agreed to expand our core team and dig deeper into the idea. We added Laura Cole, intergovernmental relations assistant, to our team. She had attended San Antonio library board meetings and met members of the library staff. Cathy Maras, chief information officer, and Construction Manager Betty Bueche joined us. Because Cole was so excited about the project, we chose her to lead it. She was transferred to the county manager's office as a special projects coordinator.

You may have noticed that nobody on our team had public library experience. I wanted it that way. I wanted fresh ideas from people who weren't encumbered by an old way of doing business. We had a well-rounded team of smart people who had technology, management, and private-sector experience. Together we could create a plan to enter the virtual world of reading and information.

We knew we would not satisfy everybody by providing only ebooks and technology, but we did have some great selling points. Ereaders were easier to carry than printed books and could be read at night without a light. Readers could mark up ebooks without permanently defacing them. They could select the size of the font and look up the definition of words by tapping the word. They could make notes. E-ink readers resemble paper and eliminate most eyestrain. Most important, ebooks would be accessible easily for our patrons because we would lend them out.

Ebooks are cost effective. They do not wear out, cannot be lost, and do not need to be destroyed. Printed books are very expensive to store, stock, index, handle, and eventually replace. We would not have to fight off bugs that stow away in books, or clean off mold, or worry about humidity and temperatures.

Printed books will always be around, and they should be. Public libraries that are providing printed books should continue to do so, but in a more cost-effective way, keeping only the most popular titles. Tom Jackson wrote an article on the Fairfax County Library, quoting Elizabeth Rhodes, the system's collection services coordinator. She said the system adds about 20,000 printed items a month and therefore must also remove 20,000 items. While some are sold or given away, many are destroyed. The article said the system destroyed 250,000 books. All libraries have the same problem.

Because Bexar County has never been in the library business, we would not be taking physical books away from our patrons. So we were likely to receive very few complaints about not having physical books.

While the Bexar County team did not include people from public libraries, we did want the advice of a forward-looking academic librarian. Academic libraries were miles ahead of public libraries in responding to technology. We found one locally in Krisellen Maloney, library dean at the University of Texas at San Antonio.

Maloney had moved most physical books off site and created a well-lighted, six-thousand-square-foot area with some two hundred computer terminals. More than 90 percent of the library collection was electronic material, and approximately 75 percent of the library's budget was spent on electronic services—compared to only 12.4 percent spent in the same category by the average public library.

We knew public libraries are much more difficult to operate than academic libraries. They serve anyone walking through door, from children to seniors. Many patrons are not as technologically astute as students are. Citizens come to public libraries for information and books and need help adapting to a digital library. We felt confident that we could meet the needs of the general public.

We became confident we were on the right track and lowered our oars deeper into the water, pulling hard to quicken the pace. By mid-October we clearly were on the road to building a digital library. We did not want the information public until we were certain we could accomplish our goals. We then would pull the library cat out of the hat and surprise everyone.

Our first location would be in a large building on Pleasanton Road on the South Side, which the county had recently opened to house offices for tax assessor-collector, constables, and justice of the peace courts. Because the building held so many government offices, hundreds of citizens already went there each day. Commissioner Chico Rodriguez also had a district office located in the building and was supportive of the idea.

The building sat in the heart of the Harlandale School District, where 92 percent of the students were Hispanic and 88 percent were economically disadvantaged. We estimated that 75 percent of the people we would serve did not have internet connections in their homes.

About four thousand square feet was available, enough room to house a main reading room, a couple of study rooms, a children's room, and a lounge. An adjacent community room also was available for civic group meetings.

In late October I asked Henry Muñoz, whose architectural firm had previously done business with the county, to do the design work for free and keep it secret. He agreed. His firm, Muñoz and Company (formerly Kell Muñoz Architects), had received numerous awards for its work, including thirty-two juried design awards. Geoffrey Edwards, who had been with the firm for more than twenty years, was assigned to the project. His work had been featured in *Architecture*, *Architectural Record*, *Texas Architect*, and other national publications.

I explained that I wanted an open floor plan, much like the setup in Apple stores. It should be a simple design that highlighted the new world of technology. He quickly went to work. On December 3 our team met at the site with Muñoz and Edwards, who said he and his team had worked all day Saturday and Sunday on the plans. He said time constraints are good because too much time leads to overthinking.

As we walked around the unfinished space, Edwards explained the layout. He wanted a futuristic feel with glass walls, curved shapes, color, and creative millwork for a contemporary look. He designed a barrel roof because a flat ceiling over the computer reading area would feel like an office space. Edwards said he wanted a bright, distinctive color to give the library a pop, making the space fun and inviting, not intimidating. He chose to create an orange soffit, or underside, connecting the barrel roof and two sides of the interior wall. He also chose orange for a long, narrow Formica counter connected to the orange checkout counter. IPad tablets would be tethered to the orange counter.

In addition to the great design, Edwards's team came up with a super name: BiblioTech. Our team came up with an owl for a mascot, giving it the name Techolote, a twist on the Spanish word for "owl." I did not like the owl idea because people erroneously think owls are smart when in fact they are not. The staff overruled me. Thank goodness they did, because Techolote became quite famous after we created a special owl suit for one of our employees to wear at events.

We designed a logo featuring an open book. Cole added wave links representing Wi-Fi and the universal symbol for on/off buttons. With that, we had a great logo and mascot to go with the name. Throughout December we refined the layout. By early January 2013 the final design was ready.

We were certain we were on the right path when another Pew Research Center report in January found that 77 percent of library patrons said free access to computers and the internet were very important. Sixty-three percent liked the idea of lending machines and kiosks located throughout the community, and 53 percent wanted a broader selection of ebooks.

While we had kept plans secret for about four months, we decided to go public before the secret slipped out. Although we still had much work to do, we held a press conference at the library site on January 10 revealing the design and announcing the digital library would open in late August. Saying we thought this would be the nation's first all-digital library, we announced that it would open with ten thousand ebooks, one hundred ereaders, forty-eight computers, and ten laptops.

Admittedly, it was gutsy to announce a library without architectural plans, without a budget approved by the Commissioners Court, with no staff, and with many unmade technology decisions. But we were confident we could pull it off.

Immediately we began to receive media attention. ABC News, the BBC, National Public Radio, the *Wall Street Journal*, and other national and international media outlets called for interviews. Thus we faced pressure not only from local constituents but also from eyes around the world. We had to perform.

On February 6, 2013, the *Wall Street Journal* published a long article on BiblioTech saying Bexar County would be the first to open an entirely digital public library. While the article was positive overall, it did quote skeptics who said patrons would insist on printed books. In May a reader from Liskeard, Cornwall, named Sigi wrote in response to a BBC News report on BiblioTech, "I have worked in libraries for fifteen years. I think people should think less about libraries as buildings in which to house books and more as places to access and disseminate information and knowledge. If you want hard copies or paperbacks, you should visit a bookstore or plan a trip to an archive. A paperless library would allow users to access information quickly at their convenience." We could not have said it better.

After the press conference, we were hanging in the wind to be battered if we did not deliver. We had about eight months to produce what we promised or crawl back in a hole. We met with the project design team on February 5 after gathering information from our technological and operation teams. Edwards had all the information he needed to move forward with architectural plans. On April 12 we cracked the front wall to begin construction. Although we had not received all the subcontracting bids, we started anyway. No doubts remained about whether we would build the digital library.

While we were creating a cool space, we also needed to furnish it correctly. On Wednesday, April 3, our team went to the Office Solutions showroom located on Broadway near downtown. We chose slate mesh-back, armless roller chairs and desks with laminated white tops and platinum metal frames. For the two study rooms, we chose height-adjustable conference tables with surface integrated power wire management. For the lounge, we chose four modern two-seat couches and a modular seating system with small tables for the laptops and iPads. In the children's area, we chose Runtz ball chairs and beanbag loungers.

The Commissioners Court approved a budget with the understanding that Tracy would raise private funds to cover some of the costs. I had asked her to raise the money through the Hidalgo Foundation, of which she was president. She quickly set up a plan to raise $500,000.

I visited the job site frequently and found that work was proceeding slowly. At that pace, I did not believe we would meet our timeline. On July 15 I pulled construction team members together and told them they were working banker's hours. I said we needed new leadership. Dan Curry, the county's capital projects manager, said he personally would take over the project. As we rushed construction, we also made decisions on technology, an ebook supplier, a librarian, and a team of techies to run the library. We were running faster than rabbits.

In essence, we were building a retail store, and to be successful, we needed products that consumers wanted. Apple offered the branding and quality of products that consumers were buying in record numbers. Washington-based Dave Levy, national sales manager for Apple, was assigned to our account. I knew Apple was not an altruistic company eager to provide free assistance or give donations. Steve Jobs was no Bill Gates, and his successors maintained his policy. The best I could hope for was a top Apple team to work with and, perhaps, a better price.

I did not get good vibes from Levy. When I mentioned that the digital library would garner a lot of attention and free advertising for Apple, he made it clear the company was not interested in publicity. Perhaps he thought we might hurt the company's image by failing in our effort to build the nation's first public digital library.

I told him our chief information officer did not want to buy Apple products because Microsoft had a better operating system. Perhaps Microsoft might appreciate an opportunity to work with us. Then he started to pay attention. He said he would personally secure the best price Apple could offer and put together a team of experts to meet with us. We met his team on June 5. Like Levy, the three team members were well over six feet tall. Height projects an aura of domination, which is symbolic of Apple's theory of fierce competition.

After they explained their plan, I turned Maras, our CIO, loose on the sky-high guys. She raised concerns about the cost and services of Apple products and the difficulty of fitting them into her existing system. She gained traction as the meeting continued, and they agreed to a better price.

Maras then assigned leaders from her team to integrate the Apple consumer products into our internet technology business enterprise. While BiblioTech would operate on its own network, it needed to connect to the county's network to access internet and intranet sites. Maras made the two divergent paths come together seamlessly to create a "wow" technology. She purchased fifty twenty-seven-inch iMac computers—two extra in case of any failures; seven MacBook Pros; and forty iPads. She also obtained software to wipe the computers, laptops, and iPads clean after each patron's use and installed a high-speed Wi-Fi network for laptops and tablets.

Cole had spent months analyzing potential ebook distributors. She was impressed when 3M Library Systems announced a major rollout of ebook services in a partnership with Polaris Library Systems. She began to zero in on 3M. Polaris had designed software that was a step ahead of other integrated library systems, bringing library resources into one convenient interface. Polaris's partnership with 3M Cloud Library would offer the industry's first fully integrated ebook catalog, allowing library patrons to discover, check out, and place holds on ebooks without ever leaving the Polaris library catalog. This met the goal of the Readers First Initiative, a group of three hundred libraries representing 200 million readers who wanted an easy library patron experience.

3M also had its own ereader, a simple, durable device that could be used only with its downloaded ebooks. The ereader could keep a battery charge long enough for the two-week loan period and could be recharged only with equipment from the library. Cole and her team decided to go with 3M. On March 3 the

Commissioners Court approved a contract making the company our ebook provider. That same day the court approved $250,000 to purchase approximately ten thousand books.

When we signed with 3M, the company offered between 175,000 and 200,000 titles through two hundred publishers. Now it has more than 350,000 titles and one thousand publishers and keeps adding content. Unlike other ebook providers for public libraries, 3M allowed us to own the digital content unless a publisher restricted a particular book to a specific time period. If the library left 3M, it could move its content to another platform, and it was not required to sign a multiyear contract. The company also had Discovery Terminals, portable kiosks that would allow patrons to browse BiblioTech's ebook collection from places other than the library. We would eventually use these kiosks in multiple locations around the county, including the jury room in the courthouse, the three military libraries, and VIA Metro bus transfer stations.

On June 20 officials of the Texas State Library and Archives Commission gave our library a provisional accreditation. This was important because it allowed the library to tap into TexShare, a program that includes $49 million in subscription databases shared by nearly seven hundred public and academic libraries. We also could access the federal E-rate, which grants discounts for telecommunication and internet services in economically depressed areas.

We found the right librarian in Ashley Eklof. With bachelor's degrees in English literature and language studies and a master's degree in library and information science, she had six years of experience in public and school libraries. She was also willing to move from Wisconsin to Texas to join the team. We then hired

Catarina Velasquez as branch manager. She had been active in the community providing job training for adults, employment opportunities for youth, and health and wellness initiatives.

Cole set up shop in a downtown county office building next to the courthouse. Working with Eklof and Velasquez, she began assembling a team. Apple sent four people to help set up the system, test it, and acquaint our team with the hardware. With leadership in place, design of the website began. The library team worked with Maras and her group to design it. The resulting product was attractive and easily navigated.

A new Pew Research Center report arrived, providing confirmation that some of the most avid library users were going less often to library branches and more often to library websites for book and audio downloads.

We began moving into the building just two weeks before it was completed. Maras assigned eight employees to help set up the equipment and test it on site. Apple engineers joined them. The team also set up a digital art and information system on five separate screens. A large screen in the hallway leading to the library features a welcome message, as well as points of interest about BiblioTech. In the children's room, Maras licensed Kaplan educational software for eight interactive learning games to be played on the four Microsoft Surface tables. She also purchased three large screens for Xbox interactive games.

We missed the August opening by ten days. In early September a soft opening extended over five days. Twenty-nine civic and educational institutions took tours to see how the library system operated. We showed them icons on the home screens that would take patrons to sites holding incredible amounts of information, including the Digital Public Library of America,

World Public Library, Google Books, Project Gutenberg, UTSA's library, Mango Languages, and Atomic Learning, which provides technology training.

We also had a special event organized by my wife, Tracy, for contributors to BiblioTech. NuStar CEO Bill Greehey, standing in front of the donor wall, spoke about the importance of his early use of public libraries. Tracy exceeded her goal of raising $500,000 for BiblioTech, led by donors Bill Greehey, David Zachry, and Gary Joeris.

During the soft opening NBC News visited the library and produced two stories for the *Nightly News* and the *Today Show*. Later Fox News, CBS Evening News, and media outlets from the Netherlands, France, and several other nations also produced stories.

Grand opening day, September 14, was a hot Saturday morning. I mean really hot. A bright sun bore down on the large stage set up in the parking lot. Behind the stage a green and blue acrylic lighted sign above the front door spelled out "BiblioTech" in twenty-four-inch uppercase letters. More than two hundred people gathered for the opening.

Apple officials attended but asked us not to mention them. They still had doubts about us. Months later, after they saw we were successful, Apple's marketing team set up a photo shoot to use the library in its marketing materials. We politicians call that catching the late train, referring to supporters who show up after you win.

Rackspace CEO Graham Weston had accepted my invitation to be the keynote speaker. While people were gathering outside, I showed him around inside. As he walked through the library, he got caught up in the excitement of the project. He used the

Discovery Terminal to find several ebooks that he downloaded to his iPad.

Tracy came inside and said, "You and Graham need to stop talking and come outside. The pavement is hot. Get started before someone has a heat stroke."

In his opening remarks before the sweating crowd, Weston said, "This world-changing idea came into being, not in Silicon Valley, New York, or Tokyo, but right here in Rackspace's own backyard, San Antonio, Texas.... It's a cloud library built on a scalable, high-performance foundation SaaS. As Marc Andreessen might say, software has eaten the library. Is it possible that Judge Wolff just made libraries...cool?" We then pressed a giant power button on the front of the podium. The doors to BiblioTech slid open, and confetti came pouring out.

Dressed in my gray BiblioTech shirt with white stripes and our blue-and-green logo on the sleeve, I joined the rest of the team in the library to greet its new patrons. Helping us were fifteen volunteer "Techolotes" in BiblioTech T-shirts. A long line of people gathered to sign up for library cards, then checked out ebooks and borrowed ebook readers.

In the children's area kids played on the three Xbox Kinect consoles and four interactive Surface table games. In the main reading room, everyone tried out the computers. A quartet from the San Antonio Symphony played for patrons as they waited in line to register. The Spurs Coyote entertained kids in the conference room as we gave away drawstring bags, T-shirts, pens, pencils, and cookies with our logo.

The day was very busy. More than 1,150 people came through the doors, and 500 registered for library cards on that day alone. Patrons checked out more than 500 ebooks, as well as 65 ereaders.

After the opening we wasted no time planning the next step. Four months later we opened a satellite site in the jury room of the Justice Center. Each year some seventy-five thousand potential jurors wait in this room until they are released or assigned to a court. We built a counter and installed a Discovery Terminal in a small nook at the back of the room. We check out ereaders or help people download books to their personal electronic devices. This has proved a cost-effective way to reach new patrons. Over the years thousands of potential jurors have signed up for library cards and used library services.

In March 2014 we took another step. In a small room, deep within the jail, I greeted two young mothers dressed in jailhouse uniforms as they walked into the room with their children. They were excited when we gave them ereaders loaded with about 150 children's books. I listened to them as they read to their children.

Next we developed a program to work with Bexar County Adult Probation to offer basic technology classes to probationers who wanted to make positive changes in their lives. Our trained BiblioTech staff taught skills such as email use, document storage, and document presentation to eager learners. Probationers graduated from the six-week training class with completion certificates, technology skills to assist in obtaining employment, and a genuine sense of pride and accomplishment.

In May my wife, Tracy, announced that the Hidalgo Foundation would make a $120,000 grant to BiblioTech to purchase one thousand ereaders to give to public school libraries. In fall 2014 our staff began going to schools to provide technical assistance to librarians and to introduce our collection of ebooks, magazines, and periodicals to students. We started with South San Antonio School District. At an event at South San High School on September 18, we delivered Nooks and Kindles to the district's school librarians. District officials were so encouraged that they bought an additional 150 devices.

We also established our school library programs in the Harlandale, East Central, Alamo Heights, Northeast, North Side, Southwest, Fort Sam Houston, San Antonio, and Edgewood school districts. Eventually we were in fifty-eight school libraries.

In July we entered into a partnership with the Warrior and Family Support Center at Fort Sam Houston, which provides a homelike environment where wounded warriors can access services. We introduced wounded warriors to the library and registered them for library cards. Each computer in the center was imaged for direct access to all the library's collections.

On September 13, 2014, we celebrated the library's first anniversary with a cool event at BiblioTech. The library team produced a ninety-second Newbery film based on the book *A Single Shard*, featuring children using equipment from the library. A youth dance group from the Korean American Cultural Center of San Antonio performed an inspiring dance, with each young person playing a drum and dancing with fans.

During its first year of operation, 103,974 patrons visited the library. Patrons checked out 76,659 ebooks, and our ereaders were circulated 6,464 times. We also organized 160 community events to engage families in reading. In 2014 *Government Technology* magazine named me one of the nation's top twenty-five Doers, Dreamers, and Drivers for taking the lead in creating BiblioTech. The March/April 2014 issue of *Public Libraries,* the magazine of the Public Library Association, featured an article by BiblioTech library executive Alicia Hays, "The Nation's First Digital Public Library."

Cole and Eklof presented the story of BiblioTech to Dutch library directors in Utrecht, Netherlands, in March 2014. Cole also was the keynote speaker at an international conference on public libraries in the digital age in Birmingham, UK, in August.

But all was not rosy regarding BiblioTech, as supporters of the San Antonio Library saw it as a threat to their library system. In the 2014 November general election, I found out how controversial disruptive technology can be when it threatens the status quo. My Republican opponent, Carlton Soules, a former city council member, teamed up with some of the supporters of the San Antonio Public Library. Soules said he opposed BiblioTech and would stop it in its tracks if he were elected.

I felt betrayed after my strong support for the San Antonio library system as mayor and then as county judge. During my terms as county judge, the county had given the San Antonio Library more than $30 million. San Antonio library supporters should have supported BiblioTech's effort to bring more reading opportunities to citizens. Despite their efforts I beat my Republican opponent by eight points.

Elections do count. In summer 2015 the county opened a second BiblioTech in the San Juan Gardens on Zarzamora Street on the West Side. Tenants of the redeveloped complex include those able to pay market rent and those who need subsidies. The San Antonio Housing Authority provided a 2,100-square-foot commercial space within the complex of 539 units for an annual rent of one dollar.

We named the library after Ricardo Romo, who was president of UTSA for many years. He grew up on the West Side and graduated from the University of Texas at Austin, where he was the first UT student to crack the four-minute mile on the track. The great thing about a digital library is that any space can be configured to provide digital books and information. We had only one study room and no large lounge, but we still installed forty computers and created a children's area. Green space and a porch outside allowed for benches and tables with access to Wi-Fi.

In December 2015 we partnered with three local military libraries, delivering 150 ereaders, three Discovery Terminal kiosks, and digital resources. Military personal based in San Antonio had access to our resources even when they were in Afghanistan, Iraq, or anywhere else in the world.

The following year we announced that we would open a third BiblioTech branch in a new SAHA housing project in the East Side Promise Zone. In what is expected to be a transformational project featuring more than five hundred units, there will be a mix of market and subsidized housing. The housing authority will provide library space, just as it did for the West Side library. This library will have more than four thousand square feet, a little more than the South Side location.

In fall 2016 we entered into a partnership with VIA Metropolitan Transit Authority, locating BiblioTech kiosks in their transfer stations to make books and information available to transit riders. VIA installed Wi-Fi on all its buses, enabling patrons to read while riding.

On December 15 we launched a partnership with University Hospital, installing a kiosk in the hospital lobby. We plan to expand to all of their locations. Every patient and visitor will find books and information available to them through the hospital's Wi-Fi.

In December 2016 we teamed up with US Representative Will Hurd to launch a program at BiblioTech to train teachers to teach coding in middle school. Hurd, who has a CIA background, had been instrumental in supporting cybersecurity efforts.

In June 2017 BiblioTech acquired CloudLink and entered an interlocal agreement with eleven other Texas libraries, giving BiblioTech patrons access to an additional 33,000 ebooks and audiobooks and bringing our total to 74,000 ebooks. The shared content resource also increased our library's circulation by over 76 percent in the first month alone.

BiblioTech has expanded its prerequisite classes to include the Open Cloud Academy, makerspace, robotics, introduction to coding, music theory using digital technology, and general technology classes. Upgraded ebook readers include the Nook and Kindle, and a Wi-Fi hotspot check-out program provides Wi-Fi access to citizens to be used with their personal computer and mobile devices.

On the morning of April 19, 2018, more than four hundred citizens gathered in and around an open-air tent to kick off the opening of BiblioTech East. Based on the recommendation of Antioch Missionary Baptist Church pastor Kenneth Kemp and my constituent services director, Dwayne Robinson, we named the library after former Antioch pastor Reverend E. Thurman Walker.

Walker's widow, Jo Angelia Walker-Waters, delivered remarks that captured the essence of the library's mission. "Pastor Walker used to tell our children that knowledge is power," she said, "and if you can read, you can do anything your heart desires." She added: "Access is power. In this digital and virtual age of technology, people need access to be included and informed."

After a few more speeches, former Spurs basketball player Sean Elliott led us into the county's largest usable space digital public library. Commissioner Tommy Calvert, Tracy, and I set off confetti as the doors swung open. The library contained fifty computers, a children's area, two study rooms, a conference room, and a makerspace with 3D printers and filmmaking and robotics equipment.

Tracy had raised $1 million for BiblioTech East, including donations from Harvey Najim, Peter John Holt and his sister, Corinna Holt Richter, the Kronkosky Foundation, H-E-B, Toyota, the Spurs Foundation, and the Freeman Coliseum Board.

BiblioTech Director Laura Cole selected Tivy Whitlock, who has a master's degree in adult and higher education and is a doctoral student at the University of Texas at San Antonio, to manage the library. More than three thousand patrons visited BiblioTech East in the first two weeks.

As of the opening, the library's website has had 1.26 million visitors; 515,000 patrons have visited our first two libraries, and 514,000 ebooks and 17,000 ebook readers have been checked out. We now have three full-time librarians—Cole, Alena Engstrom, and Elizabeth Tarski McArthur, who took the place of Eklof when she moved to another city.

Born into the world of disruptive technology, BiblioTech has not only survived its critics' arrows but has also prospered, expanding the world of reading and technology for its patrons. BiblioTech is positioned for future innovations to bring the best of technology, information, and books to the public.

# *Conclusion*

THE LARGEST ECOLOGICAL RESTORATION of a river in an urban setting; a setting for the story of the confluence of cultures along the historic San Pedro Creek; a World Heritage Site designation for our Alamo and missions; a state-of-the-art Tobin Center for the Performing Arts; a gleaming Sky Tower hospital taking health care to a new level; development of a therapeutic justice system to help people with drug addiction and mental health issues rather than incarcerating them; an evolving high-tech industry; and a new way to read and access information and technology through BiblioTech. In this book you have read about these initiatives, but what do they collectively say about our city?

Collectively they represent our city's vision for protecting and enhancing our environment; our commitment to remembering and celebrating our heritage; our love of the arts and our appreciation of its significant contribution to our city; our willingness as a community to care for the sick regardless of their income; our support for the building of a new economy around technology; and our belief that disseminating free information digitally through the cloud will offer our citizens the tools to prosper in our new economy.

Together these six initiatives have helped lay the groundwork for the growth and prosperity of our city. Our progress was recognized nationally in October 2016 when *Forbes* published an article about the San Antonio–Austin corridor. In the article "America's Next Great Metropolis Is Taking Shape in Texas," Joel Kotkin, presidential fellow in urban futures and urban studies professor at Chapman University, called San Antonio an "emerging upstart" with a 31 percent job growth since 2000, twice that of New York City and three times that of San Francisco.

San Antonio's job growth in STEM fields is 29 percent, three times the national average, and its net domestic population increase trails only Austin among Texas cities. Its cost of living is significantly lower than that in other Texas cities, and it ranked in the top ten cities (nearly even with Austin) for attracting educated millennials. In the 2016 Business Facilities annual ranking report, the San Antonio metro area was ranked first in economic growth potential. The following year a *Forbes* report recognized the San Antonio area as one of the best at creating high-wage jobs. We ranked sixth in the country with high-wage jobs, growing 17.2 percent from 2011 to 2016. From 1990 to 2016 the San Antonio metro area had an employment growth of 88 percent, exceeding all Texas cities save Austin. On a monthly basis, year-over-year employment growth has averaged 2.4 percent. As of December 2016, 1,030,000 are employed.

While our overall growth in prosperity has been impressive, it has also been uneven. We have not yet been able to even out the economic disparity between the North Side and the inner city. Although our efforts to encourage inner-city growth have sown seeds and shown early gains, we still have a long way to go. There are thousands of new inner-city housing units in all price ranges, yet inner-city jobs still have not grown as fast as necessary to reach some level of equality. We have laid the groundwork for further job development in the inner city with the evolving tech industry, Brooks City-Base, Port San Antonio, and possible Toyota expansion.

Education still continues to baffle us. In Bexar County about 260,000 people have taken some college courses and another 360,000 have associate's, bachelor's, and graduate degrees, but approximately 100,000 citizens have no high school education and another 100,000 have completed only some high school.

Inner-city schools have struggled the most. They have not been able to prepare students for high-paying jobs in the new economy. Steps are being made in the right direction. Leadership in the San Antonio Independent School District is moving forward with the new CAST-Tech high school. Career and skill training classes are taking place in many inner-city schools. With effective counseling and quality instruction, we can point our young people toward these great skilled jobs.

As we continue to advance skill training and education; invest in health care, housing, and infrastructure; address criminal behavior; invest in and support the arts; and protect our environment, we will accelerate progress toward building a great city. We are on the right road but have a ways to go.

# Acknowledgments

I FIRST WANT TO THANK Tom Payton, director of Trinity University Press, for providing me great insight on the topics I have written about. Thanks also to the reviewers retained by Trinity University Press, who offered me some great thoughts that I deployed as I revised the manuscript.

Lynnell Burkett did a great job of editing the first draft of this book.

My administrative assistant, Nicole Erfurth, reviewed numerous drafts of the book and helped correct several mistakes.

Jordana Decamps, director of the Bexar County Economic Development department, provided significant insights to the chapter on technology.

David Marquez, executive director of Bexar County Economic and Community Development, gave me many ideas about how to better describe events.

My wife, Tracy, president and founder of the Hidalgo Foundation, gave me insight on the section dealing with the Children's Court.

My constituent services director, Dwayne Robinson, encouraged me to write the chapter on therapeutic justice, and it turned out to be one of the better chapters.

Suzanne Scott, general manager of the San Antonio River Authority, did a super job helping me with the chapter on the river, missions, and creek.

My chief of staff, T. J. Mayes, researched many of the topics in this book.

My executive assistant, Linda Guajardo, arranged numerous meetings with people I interviewed.

Tech Bloc founder and former Rackspace president Lew Moorman reviewed the chapter on the tech ecosystem and furnished additional information.

Rackspace Vice President Dan Goodgame contributed information on the founding of Rackspace.

Bexar County Judicial Services Director Mike Lozito had invaluable insight for the chapter on therapeutic justice.

University Health System President George Hernandez made available information for the Sky Tower Hospital chapter, and University Health System Vice President Leni Kirkman did a wonderful job reviewing the chapter.

BiblioTech Director Laura Cole provided research and help on the chapter on BiblioTech.

Bexar County Heritage and Parks Director Betty Bueche contributed research and her insight on the history of the missions.

Finally, I want to thank the staff of Trinity University Press, who made this book come to life. I also want to thank the employees of Bexar County for their dedicated work, which made the projects discussed in this book successful.

# Index

Nelson Wolff has served the greater San Antonio area as a member of the Texas House of Representatives, the Texas Senate in 1973, and the San Antonio City Council, as well as mayor of San Antonio. He currently serves as Bexar County judge, a position he was appointed to in 2001 and has since been elected to four times. During his forty-six-year tenure as a public servant, Wolff has played a key role in countless economic and community development initiatives.

CPSIA information can be obtained
at www.ICGtesting.com
Printed in the USA
LVHW012055150119
604063LV00003B/4/P